Four Square Miles
the final project

Four Square Miles

A story of pride, love, family, and a dream.

KEITH MICHAEL PRESTON

This is a work of fiction. Names, characters, places, businesses, and incidents either are the products of the author's imagination or are used fictitiously. Any resemblance to actual locales, events, or persons, living or dead, is entirely coincidental.

Copyright © 2021 by Keith Michael Preston

All rights reserved. No part of this book may be reproduced, scanned, or distributed in any printed or electronic form without permission. Please do not participate in or encourage piracy of copyrighted materials in violation of the author's rights. Purchase only authorized editions.

IBSN: 978-1-7345925-3-5

Cover Art Designed by Thomas J. Zaffo/B. DeAngelo

Typesetting & Layout by Monte Press Inc.

Printed in the U.S.A.

I am forever grateful to my spouse, Nancy Preston, my mother, Diane Preston, and father, George Preston for their continued support.

I would like to show appreciation to the following individuals for their invaluable advice and ongoing support while creating this series: Caroline Adams, Annette Nasti-Coppola, Marie Miserendino, and Amy Corcoran.

FOUR SQUARE MILES is a series that takes place in a suburb of New York City.

the final project is the last of the series.

CHAPTER 1

A lot has happened over the last few weeks and Nutsy is feeling the pressure from it. He recently made a difficult decision to operate on his own and separate from a group of local bookies he partnered with.

Because of this decision, Nutsy currently doesn't have an outlet to layoff his bets which now makes his sports gambling operation vulnerable if caught the wrong way on a game.

A few key events have gone his way though. The rumor of a fixed football game surprisingly went in his favor compared to years ago when another rumor financially ruined him.

Ladro, Nutsy's right-hand man and known thief, cleaned out Squalo's wall safe for a large amount of cash and is stashing it in the walls of his house. Nutsy gave Ladro the nod to perform the heist and hopes one day to use this cash for a family dream he is chasing.

Although some of these events have gone in Nutsy's favor, his chest is feeling tight and he's becoming concerned he might be following in his father's footsteps and may also pass away at a young age.

Nutsy's been avoiding mentioning his chest pains to his wife, but Ladro knows differently. He and Nutsy are on their way back home from visiting a new baseball complex in upstate New York and Nutsy, in a roundabout way, mentioned it to Ladro.

They visited the baseball complex because Nutsy is trying to figure out a way to make his dream profitable. He plans on pitching his local city council a proposal to develop an abandoned site located on the southeast section of his city into a state-of-the-art sports complex.

This property has been sitting vacant for many years and is close to giving way to an outside developer for condos. This developer has the backing of Leo, Squalo's son, who recently made parole because of new laws passed by the state. Leo is not a fan of Nutsy, at all, and is a man who should not be on the streets.

A few days earlier, Nutsy took a stray bullet in his shoulder while strolling on a city sidewalk with an old friend he visited for lunch. They were innocent bystanders and got caught in the middle of a local shootout.

Nutsy had his longtime friend and doctor, Munchie, remove the bullet in his office. He wanted to avoid having to explain what happened to the hospital doctors and local police. He's old school and sometimes it's not always the best way of thinking, especially now, since the gash is probably severely infected.

Munchie dug it out with office pliers and stitched it by hand without any antibiotics or pain killers, just scotch that Nutsy poured over his shoulder and then drank the rest of the bottle.

It's around 3:00pm and Ladro currently pulls over onto the shoulder of the parkway and Nutsy asks, "Jesus Christ, again?"

Ladro opens his door and replies, "Maybe you're right, I do need a rubber band."

"Just hurry up. I gotta get to the house before that prick comes back."

While Ladro tramples through bushes and brush to find a hidden spot for him to go to the bathroom, Nutsy calls his wife, Kathy. She answers the phone in the kitchen of their house and asks, "Are you almost home?"

"Soon."

"Well, hurry up. I want you here when that detective comes back."

"Where's Sammy?"

"She's in the living room."

"Put her on."

Kathy heads into the living room and hands the phone to Sammy and says, "It's your father."

Sammy answers while sitting on the couch, "Yeah, dad?"

"I want ya to be straight with me. What happened that night at the bar?"

"It was no big deal –"

"That's not what I asked ya. Do I need to repeat the question?"

"No… he made nasty comments to me and Bono, so I got mad and flipped him on his back."

"What kind of comments?"

"You don't really wanna know."

Ladro gets back into the car and mumbles, "I got shit all over me now from those bushes." He hits the gas, and they head back onto the parkway.

"Oh, I wanna know," Nutsy replies to Sammy.

"Okay, you asked… he asked us who sucks a better --"

"Whoooa! Slow down."

"You asked me, right?"

"Yeah but… alright, and then what happened after ya flipped him over?"

"I shoved my boot on his neck and told him to apologize."

"Yeah, and?"

"He did."

"And?"

"Me and Bono left the bar."

"Is that it?"

"Yeah, I swear. You can even ask Bono."

"Did you see him after that?"

"Only when he harassed me when I was walking home from school."

"Why didn't ya tell me?"

Sammy peeks toward Kathy and remains quiet since Kathy told her not to say anything to him.

"Let me take a guess. Your mother told ya not to tell me, right?"

Sammy remains quiet since she doesn't want to admit the truth that her mother had told her that.

"Well?" Nutsy asks again.

"I gotta go to the bathroom. Here's ma."

Sammy hands the phone back to Kathy and shrugs. "Just hurry home," Kathy says to Nutsy and ends the call before he can ask another question.

"Yeah sure, hang up on me next time," Nutsy mumbles to himself while sliding the phone into his pocket.

Leo paces back and forth in front of his charred shop waiting for his father to arrive. He's wondering if his body shop was purposely torched by someone. The obvious two would either be Nutsy or Ladro, or possibly Blackie for that matter. At this point, he has no clue it was his own sister that had torched it.

Belinda was desperate to get away from her father and Leo and took Blackie's advice. Since Belinda had torched the shop, Blackie gave her a job at the same bank she works at. Belinda is hoping this will start her off on a different path in life.

Squalo finally pulls up in front of the shop and Leo gets into the car. "What the hell happened?" Leo barks out.

"Walk next time. I'm doing you a favor coming down here, ain't I?" Squalo hits the gas.

"You're my father, you should."

"Yeah, lucky me… what the hell were you doing down here anyway?"

"Just had to take care of a few things."

Squalo gives him a look. He knows very well his son is up to no good. "Who do you think clipped Donolla?" Squalo asks since he is more concerned about this right now.

"Who cares? He was useless anyway."

"He was an easy vote when you needed one."

"Well, it looks like it's only you and Belo now in the group. Talking about Belo, did he push his bets onto Nutsy like you and the Weasel did?"

"I'm not sure… he said he was handling it on his own."

"Handling it on his own, ha? I thought you all went against Nutsy?"

"Yeah so?"

"Why wouldn't he just join you two?"

Squalo becomes short, "I don't know. Who do I look like, his mother? Maybe he just wanted to handle it by himself."

Leo gazes out of the passenger window trying to make sense of this situation. "Hmm."

"Hmm, what?"

"Did you notice he disappeared for a while during the game on Sunday?"

Squalo pulls over to the side of the road and slams on the brakes. "What? Just say what you wanna say."

"I'm not saying anything."

"Then what are you insinuating?"

"It just seems strange to me that Belo didn't pool his bets with you two, disappeared for a while that same night, and now the Weasel's cooked."

Squalo glances toward Leo with a curious look since his wheels are now turning.

It's currently 3:30pm and Nutsy and Ladro make another pit stop for a sandwich in a gas station convenience store.

Ladro grabs a ham and salami sandwich and Nutsy grabs a turkey wrap.

They head back toward their car parked in the parking lot and get in. Nutsy takes a glimpse of his wrap and asks, "Does this even look like turkey to you?"

Ladro peeks and replies, "Nah, more like white ham."

"What the hell is white ham?"

Ladro laughs and replies, "You know, like an old tongue."

"Just great. Thanks for the thought. I can't eat this shit now." Nutsy folds the wrap back up.

"Give it to me, I'll eat it. You can have my greasy salami." Ladro offers his sandwich to Nutsy and laughs.

"Just forget it. It was a mistake getting food there anyway."

Ladro hits the gas, and they head back onto the parkway heading south again. "This is some ride, ha? How the hell people do this every day is crazy," Ladro says.

"See? Now ya realize how good ya got it. Ya drive three blocks to The Headquarters and still complain."

"Yeah sure, I got it great. Look at us two. A thing of beauty."

Nutsy laughs and peeks at his watch. "Alright, we're makin' good time. Stop by Munchie's for a minute. I gotta get an antibiotic or something."

"I'm surprised he didn't give you one already."

"I don't think either one of us were thinkin' straight that night." Nutsy slides the back of his hand across his forehead to wipe his beaded sweat away.

Squalo and Leo are now in Squalo's apartment. The man who lives underneath Squalo just banged on his door a few times. Squalo peeks through the peephole and barks out, "You again?"

"You're ducking my calls now."

Squalo opens the door and replies, "I've been busy. What can I do for you?"

"Well for starters, how about giving me the six-grand to fix my ceiling?"

"Here's your six-grand." Squalo slams the door in his face.

From the hallway, the neighbor yells out, "You're gonna pay."

"I told you to sue me because I ain't paying for shit." Squalo struts away. Paying for the damage of his neighbor's ceiling is the least of his worries.

Nutsy and Ladro are still heading south on the Sprain Parkway. Nutsy's forehead is dripping with sweat, and his cheeks are now flush. It appears an infection is really setting in or maybe something even worse.

Ladro peeks over toward Nutsy and says, "I gotta admit, you really look like shit right now."

"That's because I feel like shit… listen, since ya promised you'd follow this through for me, I'm gonna tell ya exactly my plan in case I'm not around."

"If you're gonna talk like this, I don't wanna hear it."

"Just listen to me closely… I want a big field with bleachers and three of those… what were they called again?"

"What, the fifty by seventy ones?"

"Yeah, that's it." Nutsy wipes his forehead.

"I'm still confused though. How is this complex gonna be about kids that need special care?" Ladro's still trying to make sense of this project.

"I'm not finished… I wanna building built. One that N-J and his friends could live in… I need to know he'll always be taken care of long after me and Kathy are gone."

"You mean like a medical facility?"

"Kinda, but not for old folks like us. And last but not least, I wanna school built for them."

"A school?"

"Yeah, a place they can learn something new every day."

"This will cost a fortune, Nutsy. You want a sports park, a residence building, and a school built?"

"That's right, Ladro. If we're gonna do this, we're gonna fuckin' do it all."

"You know Leo is looking to back Miguel's condo project, right?"

"Hey, ya said ya wanna be legends, right? If so, we can't worry about those two mutts."

"One question. Where is all this money coming from? I only have eight-hundred grand in my walls right now… well, maybe less. Your sister's been hitting it."

"My sister?"

"Yeah, she's still pissed off I did the heist."

"Just move it, will ya. We can't afford to lose anymore."

"You still didn't answer me."

Nutsy replies, "If we can't get the funds from the city, we'll bring The Quad in."

"The Quad only invests in towers. There's no way they're laying out funds for a park," Ladro replies.

"Ya let me handle that… I can see it now on the billboard. The world's most famous hot dog. The Larry Tisi Dog," Nutsy sarcastically says.

"Don't start this bullshit again. I told you already. My name ain't going on no hot dog. How about the L-T fries with brown gravy?"

"Yeah sure, take Four Squares most famous four o'clock in the morning order."

"Well, I did kinda invent it."

"You? How?"

"Don't you remember we were bombed after going to the club one night, and I poured brown gravy on my fries by accident?"

"What are ya talkin' about? That gravy was for your roast beef."

"That's what I'm saying. If I didn't do that by accident, fries with brown gravy wouldn't be a thing right now."

"Why don't ya take credit for the cheeseburger deluxe with onion rings while you're at it?"

"Well, now that you mentioned it. I did kinda –"

"Forget I asked."

CHAPTER 2

Nutsy and Ladro finally make it back to their city after the grueling ride home. They walk into Munchie's office and are greeted by the secretary at a counter. "Hey, guys. I don't have either one of you scheduled for today and we're closing soon."

Nutsy replies, "We're not. I gotta see him for a minute. It's important."

"Okay, hold on." The secretary heads down a hallway since she can tell Nutsy doesn't look well. She peeks into Munchie's office to tell him that Nutsy and Ladro are in the lobby. Munchie follows her into the lobby and asks, "It's infected, isn't it?"

"How can you tell?" Nutsy asks.

"I can tell by your face… follow me."

Nutsy and Ladro follow Munchie into an examining room. Munchie turns toward Ladro and asks, "You told the nurse I said it was okay to leave the hospital?"

"Yeah, so?"

"You can't do that, Ladro. It's on file now."

"Ah relax… who gives a shit anyway?"

"I do."

"It was either that or you would've had to take my shoe out of the rhinoceroses' mouth."

Munchie has a confused look and asks Nutsy, "What's he talking about?"

Nutsy replies, "I don't know. He said some guy was snoring like a rhinoceros in the next room."

"You should've heard this guy. I felt like I was on a safari or something."

"Yeah, Indiana with a bandage on his head," Nutsy sarcastically says.

Munchie shakes his head and hands Nutsy a slip. "Bring this to the pharmacy and take it all… and no drinking with this medication either."

Nutsy's eyes roll, and Munchie continues, "I'm serious. This stuff is potent."

Ladro cuts in, "Do me a favor, take his blood pressure."

"For what? It's always been good," Munchie replies.

"Just do it," Ladro replies. He has a gut feeling Nutsy's pressure is sky high.

Munchie picks up a blood pressure sleeve from a table.

Nutsy says, "I don't have time for this shit right now."

Ladro replies, "Just fucking do it already."

Nutsy rolls his eyes while Munchie tightens the sleeve around his bicep and pumps it a few times. Munchie pumps again, listens. He pumps again, listens. Munchie removes the sleeve and sighs.

Nutsy shrugs while waiting for the results.

"I noticed a hesitation," Munchie says with a concerned look.

"Hesitation? Like what, my heart took a break or something?"

"Yeah, like a skip."

"I knew something wasn't right. He keeps grabbing his chest," Ladro says.

"You guys are both fuckin' nuts." Nutsy rolls down his sleeve and slips on his jacket.

"What are you grabbing your chest for?" Munchie asks.

"Just a little agita. We went over this already with the chicken and broccoli, remember?"

"Agita?"

"Yeah, we're Italian. We get agita, don't we?"

"I think we should look into this further," Munchie replies.

"I'll be fine." Nutsy heads toward the door.

"I wouldn't be as concerned if your father didn't die at an early age from heart problems."

This comment got Nutsy's attention. He turns back and asks, "Why, ya think I have what he had?"

"I have no idea, Nutsy. We just know he died young from heart issues," Munchie replies.

Ladro chimes in, "I think you should get checked out. Years back, no one knew anything until they dropped dead. At least now you can get some tests run."

Nutsy sighs and stares at the wall. This has been on his mind lately since he's been feeling tightness in his chest. He never wanted to believe he could have any issues like his father had, but the twinges in his chest are becoming too frequent for him to ignore anymore.

"What do you think?" Munchie asks.

Nutsy hesitantly replies, "Alright, set up whatever ya need to. Ladro, come on." Nutsy heads out of the room.

Ladro says to Munchie, "Set it up as fast as you can before he changes his mind." Ladro follows Nutsy out of the office.

Nutsy and Ladro are now heading north on the main avenue when Nutsy peeks at his watch. "We got twenty minutes. Stop by Mucci. We gave him enough time to square up."

They pull up in front of Mucci's store and get out of the car. They both enter the beer distributor and Mucci nervously says while standing behind a counter, "I only have half. Sorry."

"Ya know something, Mucci. You were bustin' my balls when I capped ya and now ya can't even pay that."

"In a way, I'm glad you did cap me," Mucci replies.

"Good, because the other half I'm gonna take with six months of kegs for Sista."

"That's worth a lot more than what I owe you."

"Then maybe you'll learn next time." Nutsy heads out of the store.

Mucci says to Ladro, "This is crazy. That's worth double what I owe him."

"What can I tell you? And make sure to send over the premium stuff. Not that cheap, watered down shit you've been sending over lately." Ladro walks out.

Ladro pulls up in front of Nutsy's house at 4:50pm. "Thanks for takin' a ride," Nutsy says while stepping out of the car.

"I have to say, it was an adventure."

Nutsy laughs and closes the door. He heads into his house and is greeted by Kathy in the foyer. "I'm glad you're back. I didn't want this guy coming again without you here."

"Did he look familiar?"

"Yeah, he's the detective who had a crush on Blackie."

"I knew it." Nutsy strolls into the living room where Sammy lies on the couch with the ankle wrap on.

Binky is eating Chicken Cacciatore at the bar in his restaurant when Miguel approaches behind him. Miguel places a thick white envelope on top of the bar and says, "This is from my workers. Some fix, ha?"

Binky shoves the envelope inside his jacket and shrugs.

"We need to talk," Miguel says.

"Yeah, what's up?" Binky takes a swig from his whiskey glass to wash down the bite he just took.

"I lost one of my key investors and I'm looking for a replacement. I thought maybe you might be interested."

"In what?"

"I got a big condo development close to getting approved up the line."

"Where?"

"Four Square."

"Four Square? Where in Four Square?" Binky takes another swig from his glass.

"The old stadium park on the south side."

"Isn't Nuccio trying to rehab it?"

"Yeah, but that ain't never gonna fly. Four Square is going broke as it is. Besides, it looks like things will be changing up there."

"I heard you've been running around with that degenerate the state just released."

"A little here and there, why?"

"You're making a big mistake running around with that guy… is he backing you too?"

"He's trying to get the funds together."

Binky takes a swig from his whiskey glass and replies, "Thanks for keeping me in mind. I want no part of that fucking guy."

"I'm only asking for investors, not workers."

"Yeah, good luck with that one." Binky knows that if Leo is involved, trouble isn't too far behind. Besides, he's hoping Nutsy gets the deal since he and Nutsy have an agreement in place already.

"Well, if you change your mind, let me know." Miguel turns and walks away.

"Who did you lose anyway?" Binky is curious.

Miguel turns back. "Big Charlie."

"Ah, he'll probably change his mind. Him and Leo were joined at the hip years back."

"They already met, and things didn't work out too well. Don't count on seeing Big Charlie anymore." Miguel walks out.

Nutsy sits at the island in his kitchen and calls his attorney, Marcus. Marcus answers the phone while sitting in his office on 1st street, "Hey, Nutsy."

"Let me ask ya a question. That prick Dons wants to question my daughter about something. What should I do?"

"About what?"

"They found some young punk in the woods the other day."

"I heard the same thing. Why her though?"

"Apparently, she had an issue with him at a bar one night."

"Is he taking her in?"

"No, he's coming to my house now."

"I'll be right there." Marcus hangs up and races out of his office.

About ten minutes later, the doorbell rings at Nutsy's house and Kathy answers the door. Detective Dons stands on the step and asks, "I gave you a little extra time. Is your husband back?"

Nutsy appears behind Kathy with a stern look. "Yeah, what can I do for ya?" Although Nutsy feels horrible, he still needs to appear tough, especially around this crooked detective.

"I told you. I need to ask your daughter a few questions."

Marcus parks his car in front of Nutsy's house and races toward Nutsy's front door. Detective Dons notices Marcus and asks, "What is he doing here?"

"He wants to listen. Why, ya gotta problem with it?"

"No. Let's get this over with," he replies with an annoyed look.

FOUR SQUARE MILES, *the final project* 21

They all enter Nutsy's dining room and sit down. Sammy limps into the room and takes a seat next to Kathy. Detective Dons takes out a small pad from the inside of his jacket and asks, "What happened that night between you and Vito?"

Marcus cuts in, "Did he go missing from that night?"

"No."

"Then why does it matter?"

"Because I need to establish if there were any issues with the two of them."

Nutsy cuts in, "Well, you and I had issues back in the day. Does that matter now?"

"This is different."

"Oh yeah, how so?"

"A young man was found beaten and dumped."

"What are ya insinuating, my daughter did it?"

"I'm not. Are you?"

"I'll tell ya what. Pick your scraggly ass up and get the fuck outta my house." Nutsy never cared for this guy one bit.

"I'll just bring her in if I have to."

"Nutsy, let him ask," Marcus says since he would rather the questioning be done here than at the precinct.

"He said some really nasty things to me and my friend," Sammy says.

"Like what?"

Sammy glances toward her father and Nutsy shrugs. "Go ahead. Tell 'im."

"He asked us who sucks a better –"

Nutsy cuts in, "Alright... I can't let her say it. I think ya get the point here."

Blackie enters the house and pauses when she sees Detective Dons. "What's this asshole doing here?"

"Good to see you again too, Blackie."

Blackie cannot stand Detective Dons either. When she was involved with the illegal group years back, he would purposely book her to try and sleep with her. While on their way to the police station, he would tell her that they could make other arrangements before he brought her in. She never took him up on any of his crude offers.

The bookings became almost a monthly event and after Detective Dons realized Blackie would not bite on any of his offers, he made sure to pat her down thoroughly.

Once Nutsy got wind of this, he made sure Dons' classic Mustang somehow got torched. The bookings stopped shortly after that but not without further tension between Nutsy and Dons.

This led to the deal between Dons and Leo. Leo knew of the heist that Ladro and his brother were going to perform together and thought it was a great opportunity to take

Ladro out. That was the day Ladro's brother died since he took the kill shot intended for Ladro.

To this day, the case is still unsolved, but everyone believes it was Leo who pulled the trigger. In any case, Dons is still seeking his payment for the hit.

Leo believes he doesn't owe the money to Dons since the wrong person was taken out. Besides, Leo doesn't have that amount of cash anymore.

Detective Dons finishes his questioning with Sammy and abruptly leaves without even a goodbye or a thank you. Nutsy seemed content listening to Sammy's answers but still doesn't trust what this crooked detective is capable of manipulating.

CHAPTER 3

The next morning, Leo's phone rings while he's sitting in his father's living room and he answers, "Hello."

The claim rep who is handling the investigation of his burnt shop asks, "Is this Leonardo DeSanto?"

"Yeah, who's this?"

"I'm calling from Texco Insurance Company regarding the investigation of your store."

"Yeah and?"

"Well, sir, we checked and have no record of the payment."

"So, you're taking the broker's word over mine?"

"Unless you have a receipt for the cash, there's not much we can do."

"Who gets a receipt for cash?"

"Well, sir, that's why we always recommend paying with a check. At least it's postmarked by the post office."

"Why does that matter?"

"Because if a payment gets delayed, we'll sometimes honor the postmark if it was mailed well in advance."

"Is that so?"

"Yes, I wish I had better news for you. Good luck."

"Yeah, me too." Leo ends the call and yells out, "I got it!"

Squalo strolls in from the kitchen holding a coffee mug. "You got what?"

"Does Benny still work in the post office?"

"How the fuck am I supposed to know?"

Leo wanders onto the terrace and calls his sister. Belinda answers her phone while sitting at a desk in the bank. "Yeah, Leo?"

"I need to see you. Where are you?"

Belinda hesitates. She was not ready to tell Leo she is working at the bank this soon.

"You still there?" Leo questions.

"Yeah… I'm working at a bank now." She figures she has no choice but to tell Leo.

"What bank?"

Belinda hesitantly replies, "The same bank Blackie's at."

"This is a joke, right?"

"I had to do something when the shop burnt down, and they had an opening."

"What time you there till?"

"Four."

Leo hangs up the call and heads back into the apartment.

An hour later, Leo enters the bank and notices Belinda sitting by a desk off to the side of the room. She immediately sees him and stands up to greet him. Well, not exactly, she wants to beat him to the punch. "Hey, good to see you."

Leo stares for a moment. He wonders why she is so cordial to him. Maybe this is part of her job, or maybe there's more to this. "This is something, ha?"

"What is?"

"The ashes are still smoking, and you already got a job."

"What can I say? They needed someone and I need the cash."

"You? How about me?"

Blackie notices Leo from her office window and shakes her head. She knew it was just a matter of time until he popped in to show his face. She didn't think it would be this soon though.

Belinda and Leo take a seat by Belinda's desk. Leo glances around. He catches eyes with Blackie and gives her a wink. "So, what is it?" Belinda asks.

"I need you to write out a check and date it, September eighteenth."

"A check for what?"

"My insurance."

"Dad said he was taking care of it."

"Well, he didn't. And the insurance lapsed."

"There's no coverage?"

Leo shakes his head no.

"Then you write it out."

"I can't. It needs to be dated while I was in jail."

Belinda stares at Leo trying to figure out what he's up to. "Why does the date on the check matter?"

"You let me worry about that part."

"Get dad to write it then. He has the checks anyway."

"He can't. We already told the company he gave cash, and they denied the claim since we can't prove it... I'll be right back."

Blackie watches Leo strut into her office and take a seat in front of her desk. "Did I say you can sit?" Blackie asks with an annoyed look.

Leo laughs like the cocky man he is and replies, "You didn't say I couldn't either."

"What do you want? I'm busy."

"Well for starters, how the hell did this workout with my sister getting a job here?"

"I don't recall me owing you any explanations."

"Maybe not, but you still owe me the cash from that job."

"We went over this already. My husband barely made it out alive, let alone with any cash."

Leo stands up, slides a piece of paper out of his pocket, and flings it in front of Blackie on her desk. Blackie picks it up and takes a glimpse. It is a picture of a bullet sticking into a wall. Blackie flings the paper back toward Leo. "What the hell is this?"

"A picture of the day you took a shot at me."

"So?"

"I'm sure the police department could perform ballistics on it and determine what gun it was fired from."

"Your shop already burnt down."

"Yeah, but I have this picture, the bullet, and a witness."

"Yeah, who?"

"My sister."

Blackie laughs the comment off.

"You and your asshole husband got two weeks. Then I'll be expecting my cash." Leo heads out of her office without waiting for a reply.

Leo passes by Belinda again at her desk and says, "I'll be back tomorrow for you to sign the check."

"I'm not signing anything."

"We'll see about that."

Belinda sighs and watches Leo strut out of the bank.

It's now around lunch time and Nutsy and Kathy sit in one of Munchie's examining rooms together. Kathy has a concerned look about her husband's health. Besides the infection Nutsy currently has, she also noticed him grabbing onto his chest a few more times.

Munchie walks into the room and closes the door behind him. He holds up a chart to read and says, "You want the good news or bad?"

"Ya know me, Munchie. I like to hear the bad news first."

"You might need surgery."

Kathy asks, "How come?"

"It seems there's a skip. I'd like to run the test again in a few weeks."

Nutsy says, "So what. A lot of people have that shit."

"True, but we have ways to correct it today."

"How do ya know it ain't from the infection?"

"It could be, but I doubt it."

"Well, I think it is."

"Nutsy! Stop it already and listen." Kathy can already tell by her husband's questioning, that he's going to start downplaying his condition.

"Look, anything is possible. It could even be from stress. But in any case, it's currently there," Munchie replies.

"Let's see how I feel after the infection clears up."

Kathy cuts in, "If he thinks you need a procedure done, you're doing it."

"Yeah well, I gotta lotta stuff going on right now. I don't see surgery on the horizon anytime soon."

Kathy stands up. "Would you tell your father to do it if he was still alive?" Kathy is pissed off.

"My father has nothing to do with this."

"He's probably looking down at you right now wondering how much of an idiot you are questioning this."

"We'll talk it over."

"Yeah, I know your talking over. It never happens." Kathy walks out of the room. Nutsy sighs.

Later that night, Blackie is waiting for the right moment to explain to Ladro what Leo said to her at the bank. Ladro just finished watching a TV series he was engrossed in so she thought this would be a better time.

Bandit is curled up on Ladro's lap in their living room. Bandit has been getting bigger and heavier, but she still acts like a puppy and climbs all over him.

"Leo came into the bank today," Blackie says.

"I'm sure you'll be seeing more of him since Belinda is there now."

"He wants his money."

"Didn't I tell you before, I wouldn't give him the sweat off my balls?"

"He has something on us."

"Yeah, like what?"

Blackie hesitates. She knows she screwed up with the impulsive reaction she made at Leo's office. "What?" Ladro presses on.

"When you were in the hospital, I paid him a visit at the shop."

"Yeah and?"

"I used your gun and popped a round at him."

"Which one?"

"The one you had the night you hit your head."

"Oh shit, that's Nutsy's pistol."

"What the hell are you doing with it?"

"Why, what is that asshole planning on doing?"

"He has the bullet. He's threatening to go to the police if we don't pay him."

"Hold on one second." Ladro whips out his cell phone and calls Nutsy.

Nutsy answers while stretched out on a recliner watching TV in his living room, "What's up?"

"That micro nine you gave me. Can it be traced?"

"Do ya think I would hand ya something that could be traced?"

"I didn't think so… you positive, right?"

"Yeah, that came from Big Charlie when he was dumping off the rest of Leo's stock. What's going on?"

"I'll tell you tomorrow." Ladro flings his phone onto the couch and pats Bandit's head.

"So?" Blackie impatiently asks.

"You're fine. It's one of Leo's."

"Leo's? How the hell did my brother get it?"

"A fire sale when Leo got busted."

"What should I tell him then?"

"Tell him I said, he can lick my balls."

"I'm not telling him that."

"Well, tell him whatever you want. Because I ain't giving him shit."

Blackie feels somewhat relieved about this. Especially, since the bullet cannot be traced. "I'm getting rid of it. It shouldn't be in the house anyway."

"Don't. I'll hide it in the wall."

"Let's just pay him and get it over with… you have enough cash." Blackie knows Leo will never stop harassing them for the money.

"Nah, that cash is earmarked for something greater. And stop skimming it, will you?"

CHAPTER 4

The next morning, Nutsy and Ladro sit at the conference table in Marcus and Staci's office. They've been discussing Sammy's situation. Marcus doesn't seem concerned since he feels Detective Dons doesn't have a leg to stand on after hearing Sammy's side of the story, but Nutsy is a skeptic and still thinks otherwise.

"Nutsy, this guy is reaching. Why? I don't know but he is," Marcus says.

Ladro replies, "He was in bed with Leo years back. Don't be surprised if they're at it again."

Marcus replies, "If he had anything on her, she'd be in the pen right now. Trust me when I say this."

Nutsy nods in agreement. He then brings up the sports park. He has a certain vision of how he would like it to progress. Marcus says, "I have to say, Nutsy, this is a huge undertaking to get involved with."

"Let's just hope I make it to the end."

"Will you stop with this shit again?" Ladro asks.

Marcus laughs and asks, "Will the corporation be in your name?"

FOUR SQUARE MILES, *the final project* 35

"No, I don't want my name associated with it."

Staci has a confused look on her face and asks, "You're doing all this, and you don't want your name on it?"

"That's right."

"Can I ask why?"

"Because I feel my name would just be a jinx, that's why."

"I think your name on it would be the complete opposite," Staci replies.

"This park is not about me. It's about the kids. Besides, my name has too many blemishes on it and the way things are going around this city, it could have a few more."

Nutsy and Ladro are now heading toward the north side of the city. "Stop by my sister's bank for a second."

A few minutes later, Ladro pulls over in front of Blackie's bank and Nutsy gets out of the car. "I'll be right back."

"Be easy on her." Ladro told Nutsy the story about Blackie taking a shot at Leo.

Nutsy enters the bank and is immediately greeted by Belinda. "Hey, Nuccio. Good to see you."

"I didn't know ya worked here."

"Yeah, Blackie found me this job after the shop burnt down."

Blackie approaches the two of them and asks, "Wow, what brings my brother in here?"

Nutsy replies, "We need to talk."

Blackie heads into her office and Nutsy follows her in and then closes the door. "What is it?" Blackie asks.

"Listen, this is between us right now. Marcus is setting up a special needs trust for N-J and a family trust for us. What do ya need to set up an account to fund it?"

"Who's the trustee?"

"It's gonna be Kathy and Sammy."

"Why not you?"

"It's just better this way. What do you need?"

"Does Kathy know you're doing this?"

"Not yet… will ya just tell me what ya need and stop asking all these questions?"

"I need a tax ID number and the trust documents."

"Alright." Nutsy glances away. He looks like he has something serious on his mind. And he currently does.

"What wrong?" Blackie asks.

"Nothing, why?"

"I know that look very well. What's going on?"

"I need to get things out of my name. Start gettin' the papers together to change my accounts."

"To Kathy?"

Nutsy nods. Blackie doesn't continue her questioning since she can tell by Nutsy's expression something serious is twirling through his mind. He peeks toward Belinda and asks, "Does her workin' here have anythin' to do with Leo's shop burnin' down?"

"My curious brother. Always thinking things are different than what they are."

"That's because they always seem to be… and no more unnecessary trigger pulls, ya got me?"

A few weeks have gone by and Billy was able to get Nutsy in front of the city board to pitch his proposal. Billy is still sketchy about the details of the project, but he promised Nutsy he would get him an appointment, so he honored his commitment.

Nutsy first met with the mayor in her office and she loved his idea. She thought it would not only preserve the property as a sports venue, the idea of incorporating a school and home for children that need special care was brilliant.

The mayor and Nutsy head into the Urban and Planning Department office where the meeting is taking place. Six city council members sit at a long table facing the room. They are all quiet while reviewing the papers in front of them.

Nutsy never presented anything like this before in front of a board since he was always the type to stay behind the scenes. This is much different. This is his baby and only he can explain the proposal with passion. He addresses each member with a greeting and then takes a seat at a table facing them. The mayor sits off to the side and says, "You're all going to love this." She wants them to know she already has her stamp of approval on it.

Nutsy is dressed much differently than his standard sportswear look. He has on a blue suit with a white shirt. His tie is a swirl of red, white, and blue colors. His hair is groomed immaculately, and he is clean shaven. He appears calm but is rattled inside.

This is it. His one chance to make his mark in life. His chance to do something that no one has ever done before in this city. And more importantly, a chance to take care of his family's future.

He has one issue in this room though. A board member is already in bed with Miguel and has secretly backed his condo project. He was the city inspector that was trying to give Papo a hard time at one of his towers before Billy had to set him straight.

The head of the board passes sheets of paper down the row for the others to review. Sketches of the project are drawn out precisely on each page showing an outline of the grounds. Nutsy had an old friend who is an engineer draft sketches for him. The guy owed him money, so they bartered.

The mayor smiles while watching. Nutsy peeks toward her and smiles back. The city inspector catches their quick pleasant exchange and says, "It's a very heartwarming project, but I don't see it sustaining itself for the long run and that's what this city needs."

Another member who grew up with Nutsy is a retired schoolteacher and loves his idea. "I think the mayor is right. This is fabulous. Four Square could be in the record books for years if this comes to fruition."

The inspector cuts in, "Yeah sure, this project will bankrupt this city. The other condo proposal is a money maker. We've been down this road already with these sports complex proposals."

The schoolteacher replies, "Well, let's hear Nuccio explain how this will be funded and sustainable."

Nutsy nods and says, "First off, I thank ya all for this opportunity. It's been a personal dream of mine… we were hoping for a little money from the urban and planning department for a rehab project."

The inspector cuts in, "You see? And then what? We gotta keep on funding it?"

"Let him finish," the schoolteacher replies.

"If I can't get any money from the city, I have backers that are willin' to put up big money."

The inspector cuts in again, "We don't allow any illegal money to fund our city projects." The inspector is taunting Nutsy and he knows it.

Nutsy loses his cool somewhat because of this man's rudeness and says, "Who are ya kidding? Ya don't think we all know you're backin' Miguel, ha?" Nutsy stares at the inspector.

"Alright, we're getting off track here," the head of the board says.

"I come here in good faith to do something nice, something good for this city and this gentleman treats me like a piece of garbage. And I'm not likin' it one bit."

The head of the board peeks toward the inspector and says, "Not another word until he finishes."

"How about I make it easier and let you all talk?" The inspector stands up and heads toward the door.

The head member asks, "Where are you going?"

"You already know my answer." He walks out.

The schoolteacher says, "Please go on, Nuccio. I would really love to hear what you have to say."

Miguel and Leo are currently discussing business on the west side of the city. Leo tells Miguel he found a way to handle his claim and he should be able to finance the shop to invest into the condo project.

Miguel is not crazy about keeping Leo involved but doesn't know how to tell him that. Binky's comments about Leo stuck in Miguel's mind. He's just hoping at this point Leo gets busted for something again and sent back to jail. Leo answers his buzzing phone and asks, "How did it go?"

The inspector is currently standing on the steps outside of city hall and replies, "I walked out."

"Why? You were supposed to shoot down whatever he said in there."

"They love him. Even the mayor does."

"How do you know?"

"She said it. She already gave her nod."

"It figures… get your ass back in there and make him look bad, you moron." Leo hangs up with an annoyed look.

Miguel nods and Leo says, "Your guy's a fucking jerkoff."

"What happened?"

"What happened? He walked out."

"Why?"

"Who the hell knows…. bring me to the bank now."

Nutsy is still addressing the board and his pitch is going nicely. He explained that he would like one big field and three fifty by seventy fields. He had to explain exactly what the fifty by seventy fields were, since the board had no clue what he was referring to.

"I'm still confused though. This park never raised any money before. How will it with these fields?" one of the members asks.

"Travel baseball is the money driver, the part that will keep this park alive. I witnessed it myself upstate. It was a thing of beauty. Hundreds of players and families roaming around to play this great game."

"But how do we make money?" the member asks.

"Tournament ball. All the teams pay an entrance fee to play."

The retired teacher replies, "Well, my daughter played travel softball, so I have a good idea what you're referring to. Why the school and home then?"

Nutsy turns away in thought. This part has always been personal to him and never easy to discuss. Since this will probably be his only chance in front of the city council, he wants to be careful with his wording. "This proposal is unique and somethin' that no city has ever done before... and it could help take care of my son forever. Long after me and my wife are gone."

"Now it comes out. So, in a way this is personal?" the city inspector blurts out while taking his seat again.

"I might appear different on the outside, but down deep inside I'm no different than anyone else who has wishes for their families. And if the game I always loved could help this city out, then it's a win-win for us all."

The inspector sarcastically replies, "Very moving. But we're not here to fund anyone's personal wishes." He glances

FOUR SQUARE MILES, *the final project*   43

toward the board members and says, "This is a dog. A bust like the rest of the sports complex proposals."

The retired schoolteacher replies, "This is different to me. You see the fields. I see the school and the education."

Miguel pulls up in front of the bank and Leo steps out of the passenger seat. He heads into the bank and moves toward Belinda's desk. He places a business check in front of her. "Here, sign it."

"I told you already. I'm not signing anything anymore."

"We're really going down this road?"

Blackie notices Leo from her office and mumbles, "This asshole again?"

Leo says, "Alright, no problem. I'll pay your boyfriend a visit later."

"You know something, Leo. You're nothing but a coward. All you do is pick on people you know you can."

"Hey, we all do whatever it takes, don't we?"

Blackie approaches them and asks, "Is there a problem here?"

"No." Belinda reluctantly signs the check and flings it back toward Leo. "Now, get out."

Leo places an envelope on the desk and says, "Fill out the return envelope."

So, Belinda writes the shops name and address on the envelope. Blackie shakes her head and heads back into her office.

Leo snatches the envelope off her desk and says, "And get together a mortgage application. I'm refinancing the shop."

"Why?"

"I'm making an investment." Leo walks into Blackie's office and asks, "You talk to your asshole husband?"

"You think you can just walk in my office anytime you want to?"

"It's a public bank, isn't it?"

Blackie gets annoyed and replies, "Yeah, he said you can lick his balls. How do you like that?"

"Really? Okay, no problem. I'm sure the police department will love to see the bullet."

"Go ahead, show them. That bullet was fired from one of your old pistols on the street."

"You're full of shit."

"Apparently, it came from your last batch that Big Charlie was dumping for twenty cents on the dollar while you were pulling it behind bars."

"I think you're bluffing."

"Good luck. Now get the fuck out of here. Some of us actually work." Blackie sits down, picks up the phone and dials. "And don't let the door hit you in the ass."

Leo struts out without closing the door and flips the bird.

Leo gets back into Miguel's car and says, "Take me to the post office." He slams the door closed.

Miguel replies, "Leo, I gotta get back to work."

Leo slides the check into the envelope that Belinda addressed and licks the seal. "Just fucking do it."

After driving three blocks west, Miguel pulls over in front of the post office and Leo opens the door. "I'll be right back."

Leo heads into the post office and sees Benny standing behind the counter. Benny immediate gets nervous after recognizing Leo since he still owes him a favor from the past. Benny nervously stands there wondering if this is payback time. Leo pauses in front of the counter and asks, "You got a minute?"

Benny nods and says to the other postal worker, "I'm taking a five-minute break." Benny now feels this is probably the time. They both walk out of the lobby and pause by the side of the building. "What's up, Leo?"

"You know what's up."

"What do you want me to do?"

Leo hands Benny the envelope and says, "I need this postmarked, September eighteenth."

"Leo, I can lose my job doing this."

"Yeah, and I could've gotten my head busted in for helping out your brother when you asked me to."

"That was different."

"Alright, no problem. I'll consider this to be you reneging on our deal." Leo moves back toward Miguel's car.

Benny knows he cannot say no to Leo's request. Leo helped his brother years back take on a few guys in a night club parking lot that Benny had owed money to. Three guys had his brother cornered and were severely roughing him up. Benny ran inside the nightclub searching for Leo and begged him to help his brother.

Leo opens the passenger door of Miguel's car. "Leo!" Benny yells out.

Leo turns and nods. Benny approaches the car and says, "Let me have it." Leo hands him the envelope and reconfirms, "Remember, September eighteenth."

CHAPTER 5

Nutsy is still sitting in front of the city council pitching his proposal. It's been a long meeting, with a few breaks in between, and the inspector has been doing nothing but giving him a hard time every chance he gets. Nutsy has become impatient with him but advice from Billy keeps circling through his mind.

Billy had told him it could get stressful in these meetings and not every member is on board with every project. He also told Nutsy to stay calm regardless of what anyone says, since each member has their own agendas.

Billy knows one wrong move or comment and Nutsy's proposal is history. Billy also suspected that the inspector would give him a hard time and told Nutsy so.

A city council member who is intrigued by the proposal asks, "Nuccio, have you come up with a name for this park?"

Nutsy nods and replies, "I'd like to call it, Four Square Memorial Sports Complex."

"Why that name?" the member asks.

"Because there are four corners to a baseball diamond and it kinda goes with our city's name. And besides that, I feel it's important to keep Memorial in it for historical reasons."

The inspector cuts in, "Memorial is a thing of the past. We're trying to move forward, not backwards here."

"Then we have a difference of opinion. This city has been built on traditions. That park is no different –"

The inspector cuts in, "And that's why it sits there like it does. Empty and a total wreck."

"I played ball on that field. I watched turkey bowl games on that field. My wife graduated on that field. The Memorial name will never be a thing of the past for me as long as I live."

The inspector replies, "Here we go again with the personal feelings."

The mayor cuts in from the side of the room, "I agree with Nuccio. That park is a Landmark and the Memorial name should remain somehow."

The inspector puckers his lips and looks away.

After his meeting was finished, the mayor walks Nutsy to the exit of the building. She is excited about his proposal, but Nutsy feels differently. He isn't quite certain who is on the inspector's side, but the mayor feels it went extremely well. This was the first time Nutsy had ever given a proposal like this, so he has nothing to compare it to or gage it on.

They pause by the door and Nutsy asks, "How long until I know?"

"Figure a few months or so. I'll push them along."

Nutsy offers his hand for a handshake and says, "Thank you for all your help. I'll never forget this."

The mayor shakes Nutsy's hand and replies, "No, thank you for coming up with such a brilliant plan. Let's keep our fingers crossed."

"I just wish Billy was on board."

"He is, Nuccio. He can't quite grasp the concept yet, but he eventually will."

It's now around 4:00 pm and Nutsy heads into The Headquarters and takes a seat at the conference table by Ladro who is finishing up a wager call. "Yeah, you got it. Two team-tease. Giants plus nine and Philly plus three. Best of luck." Ladro hangs up from the call.

Nutsy asks, "They're teasing the same game?"

"Yeah, that's been the trend lately."

"Philly stayed at minus three against the Giants?"

"Yeah, imagine that? Forget about this shit. Long meeting, ha? How did it go?"

"I guess alright except for that inspector."

"Was he the same guy that was giving Papo a hard time with the concrete?"

"I think so."

"Where's that guy from anyway?"

"Billy thinks downtown. He's one of Miguel's clowns."

Leo and Miguel are driving on the Bronx River Parkway in the Bronx area and Miguel's phone rings through the dashboard. Miguel presses a button and ask, "So how did it finish?"

The inspector is now having a beer at a local pub and replies, "I did the best I could. Some of the members love it though."

"Will you have the majority to knock the vote down?"

"I'm not sure."

Leo cuts in, "Well, lean on them."

"It's not that easy."

"I'll show YOU how easy it is if I have to." Leo throws out a threat.

"I'll do the best I can."

"Bet your ass you will" Leo slams his hand on the dashboard to hang up the call.

"I can't believe it. They've never considered a sports park proposal like this before," Miguel says.

Leo sarcastically replies, "Sure, anything for the city poster boy."

Leo presses a number on his cell phone and waits for Detective Dons to answer. "Didn't I tell you not to call me?" Detective Dons asks while driving in his car.

"We need to talk. I'll meet you at the rubble in a half." Leo hangs up the call.

About a half an hour later, Leo and Miguel pull up in front of the charred shop. They both step out of the car and slide into Detective Dons' backseat. "Look familiar back there, Leo?"

"Yeah, fuck you too."

Detective Dons laughs and asks, "You have my money?"

"No, I'm still working on it."

"I'm getting tired of asking." Detective Dons gives Leo a nasty look through the rear-view mirror.

"Don't worry. I'll get it."

"What do you want then?"

"We need you to bust Nutsy."

"Why? He'll be back out the same day."

"I don't care if he gets out. We need him to have some bad publicity in the paper."

"Why would that matter?"

"He has a big proposal in front of the board to develop the sports park. Some bad publicity wouldn't hurt."

"What park, Memorial?"

"Yeah."

"I thought you guys had condos going up there?"

"The city has it on hold to review his plans."

Detective Dons laughs and replies, "Forget it. They'll give the golden boy anything he wants in this city."

"Well, figure something out." Leo opens the door to get out.

"I ain't figuring out shit until you square up with me."

A few days have gone by and Squalo steps out of his bathroom and enters his bedroom to get ready for the night. His clothes are already laid out nicely on his bed.

There's a knock on his front door and Squalo moves toward his foyer thinking it's his neighbor again who's been busting his balls about his ceiling. "Didn't I tell you I ain't paying –" Squalo opens the door and pauses when he sees the federal agent who Donolla was working with, standing there.

"You're not paying for what?"

"I thought you were someone else. What can I do for you, Agent Jerkoff?" Squalo recognizes him from the past.

"I see you still have a sense a humor."

"What do you want? I'm busy."

"I'm investigating two murders."

"Yeah, so?"

"One being your best friend and the other a kid from Four Square."

"Can't help you with either one."

"Not even your friend?"

"Hey look, I could be next. Maybe you should be protecting me, not questioning me."

"You picked this line of work, not me. You hear anything, you let me know."

Squalo nods and closes the door. He heads toward Leo's room and knocks on the door. "What?" Leo asks sounding like he is out of breath.

Squalo opens the door to see Leo under the covers on top of a woman in bed. "Did I say you can come in?" Leo barks out. The woman places her hand in front of her face since she is currently embarrassed.

Squalo asks, "What the fuck is this?"

"Close the door!"

"Young lady, get dressed. I need to discuss something important with my son."

Squalo closes the door and heads back toward his bedroom. "Now he thinks my place is a hotel room?" Squalo mumbles under his breath.

Leo walks the woman to the front door and opens it. "He gets crabby sometimes. I'll call you later." She walks out, and Leo closes the door behind her.

He heads toward his father's bedroom and says, "I'm trying to get fucking laid. Do you know how long it's been?"

"I don't give a shit. You ain't eighteen anymore. Go get a fucking hotel room. My place ain't your personal love shack."

"What the fuck is so important?"

"While you were playing around, a fed knocked on the door."

"For what?"

"The weasel and the punk."

"The punk?"

"Yeah, that's right. I'm telling you right now, I ain't going down with you."

"Just keep your mouth shut. You hear me?"

"I didn't have these issues before you got out. Maybe you need to go back in."

"There's no shot of that. I'll take it all down including myself before that day happens."

A month has gone by and Nutsy's infection finally cleared up. He still gets twinges here and there in his chest but not as frequently. He decided to hold off on any procedures which has annoyed Kathy to no end. She expected Nutsy to downplay his issue knowing him as well as she does, so this is not a surprise to her at all.

Ladro found out he had Lyme disease and is taking a strong dose of antibiotics. He and Nutsy have been trying to figure out where he could have gotten bit. The only explanation would be on the side of the parkway coming back from upstate since Ladro kept on stopping to go to the bathroom.

Ladro is slowly getting better and becoming his sarcastic self again. He did drag around for a few weeks with no strength at all, but the antibiotics seem to be doing the trick.

The city council is still reviewing Nutsy's plans and is torn by them. The proposal is brilliant, but they are not certain if it could sustain itself. Billy is also leaning on the board for their approval. He's using all of his pull to help push it through. Although he still can't quite comprehend the travel baseball concept, Billy feels this is probably Nutsy's one and only shot to finally get out of the rackets.

The proposal has one big baseball diamond with bleachers on the right side of the field that also wrap behind home plate giving the appearance of a mini stadium. Three additional fifty by seventy fields are included with the proposal. These modified fields will also be able to attract travel softball teams from around the country which the retired teacher loves.

Since Papo will be the general contractor of the project, he talked Nutsy into including a hotel on the far side of the large parking lot across the street from the complex. This will allow families that travel long distances to be able to stay overnight if need be. Papo wants to control and manage the hotel. Nutsy didn't mind since he's more concerned about the home and the school on the grounds.

They made a deal. Papo could manage the hotel but would have to build the school and home for the complex. The only exception is, the complex would get a percentage of the hotel sales negotiated on a yearly basis with ten percent as a base. Papo agreed since he felt this project could be a turning point for this city. This city has been lost for years. This project could help put it back on the map.

The inspector in bed with Miguel and Leo is doing everything possible to convince the other board members to knock down Nutsy's proposal since his money is backing Miguel's condo project. So far it looks like the vote is four to two against Nutsy's project.

Since there are six members, if the vote becomes even, the mayor is the deciding factor. Nutsy already knows the mayor is on his side since she is in favor of keeping this historic park as a sports complex. Leo is also aware and is doing whatever he can to stir up problems.

The federal agent also paid Belo a visit at his house. Belo seemed to do just fine with the interview and the agent is not seeking anything further from him at this time. Belo has been laying low and hasn't been around much lately.

The federal agent has now decided to pay Miguel a visit. He has information that puts Miguel, Leo, and Big Charlie together at a street corner not too far away from where Leo and Big Charlie were making their exchange.

The federal agent is now sitting in Miguel's office trying to cross items off his list, but a few things are not adding up to him. He now attempts to bait Miguel. "So, you're telling me you haven't seen Big Charlie and Leo together lately?"

"That's correct. Why?" Miguel witnessed the incident between Big Charlie and Leo and is trying his hardest to stay out of it.

The federal agent now suspects Miguel is trying to hold back information. If Miguel mentioned he did see Leo and Big Charlie it would probably make the agent think differently, but the fact that Miguel is outright lying to him, is making him think otherwise.

"I'm gonna ask you one last time. Did you or did you not see them?" the federal agent says with a serious tone.

"Nah, I got nothing for you. Sorry I can't help."

"Yeah, me too." The federal agent stands up and says his goodbye. Miguel thinks he made it through this round and is somewhat relieved.

The federal agent takes a few steps toward the door and pauses. He turns back with a photo he just pulled out from his jacket pocket and tosses it onto Miguel's desk. "Look familiar?"

Miguel takes a glimpse, and his eyes open wide. The federal agent knows by his reaction that he caught Miguel by surprise. "You look like you just saw a ghost."

"Where did you get this?"

"Does it really matter? What matters is that you're bullshitting me. And this spot happens to be around the same place Big Charlie's body was found." At this point, there are no witnesses and proof of what had happened to Big Charlie, but the agent is trying to corner Miguel.

Miguel picks up the photo and stares at it again. He knows he is in a tough spot now. He can continue to deny any wrongdoing, but he can tell by the agent's look, he feels confident in his findings and will probably continue coming at him.

Miguel decides at this point to not admit the truth until he consults with his attorney. "I don't know. Maybe I did bump into them one day. That doesn't mean anything."

"You're right, it doesn't. But if you know something and come clean, I'll make sure your deal is solid. If not, and you knew something, you're gonna take it up the ass for many years… that I'll promise you."

The following afternoon, Nutsy and Ladro stroll into The Lounge for lunch. They take a seat at the table they usually dine at in the back of the room. Nutsy has been trying to figure out how Kathy knows he has no interest in following up with Munchie regarding the discomfort in his chest.

Ladro had told Blackie and he figures Blackie might've mentioned it to Kathy, so Ladro is playing it off since he knows Nutsy will get annoyed at him. "Nutsy, I don't even remember how many cups of coffee I had this morning."

"I would say coffee and a doctor visit are a little different, ha?"

The owner approaches the table and asks, "So Nuccio, Larry, what can I get you guys?"

"You have any of the Clams Oreganata?" Nutsy asks.

"Of course."

"Good. Give me an order of those, a plate of Chicken Milanese, and a side of Ziti."

"Okay. Are you guys gonna share it?"

"Share it? No way, that's for me," Nutsy replies.

Ladro says, "I'll just have some mussels, Chicken Marsala, Ziti, and a Cold Antipasto."

Nutsy sarcastically ask, "Oh, that's it?"

The owner laughs and ask, "How about coffee?"

"Not for me. I had five cups already," Ladro replies.

"Oh, now ya remember how many cups of coffee ya had?"

"Nutsy, I told Blackie. That's it. I'm telling you it wasn't me that told Kathy."

"Not directly but indirectly."

"Alright, it was me. You feel better now?"

"Not really."

"Jesus Christ. You're never happy."

Nutsy just laughs.

CHAPTER 6

Kathy has been pestering Nutsy about his follow up consultation with Munchie since Nutsy has still been downplaying his condition. He has been blaming the infection for why he was getting discomfort in his chest, but Kathy knows it started well before that time.

They are currently in Perrotto's Deli on the main avenue buying cold cuts for the week. "Nutsy, don't start this again. It was happening way before the infection," Kathy says while waiting for their order to be rung up.

"I know exactly what I need."

The owner hands a big brown bag to Nutsy and one to Kathy and says with an Italian accent, "You enjoy a this. I put a little extra for a the kids."

"You've always been a good man. How much do I owe ya?" Nutsy asks.

"You a pay me later, Nuccio. You wife looks a beautiful today, like a always."

Kathy replies, "Thank you. That's kind of you."

"He a lucky man."

"Yeah, I know that. Thanks again," Nutsy replies while walking out of the store with Kathy.

They both head down the avenue toward their parked car. "I get more compliments from the store owners than I do from you," Kathy says.

"You already know I think you're beautiful, right?"

"That's not the point."

"Ya complain I say things over and over... but I guess for this, it's okay." Nutsy laughs it off.

"A little bit of affection once in a while won't kill you."

"How do ya know that? I'm sure it killed a few men."

"I hate it when you start acting this way. You sound like a real idiot."

Nutsy laughs then suddenly pauses since he got a sharp twinge in his chest.

"Affection won't kill you, your stupidity will first."

"I'm fine. Come on," Nutsy replies and starts heading down the sidewalk again.

Kathy continues walking with Nutsy and replies, "You're going back to Munchie. I don't wanna hear it anymore."

"I told ya already. I know exactly what I need."

"And that is?"

"I gotta change my ways. I wanna see if that helps first."

"And how are you gonna do that?"

"I'm gonna stop drinking, smoking cigars, and maybe even cursing."

"Now I know you're really bullshitting me."

"Nah, I'm gonna try it first… I think it might do the trick."

"That doesn't make any sense. This is a condition, not a lifestyle."

"You know and I know, half of people's problems are from stress and how they treat their bodies."

Kathy shakes her head. She feels this is Nutsy's way of procrastinating and her husband is making up excuses again.

It's a few hours later and Nutsy is strolling down the street with Papo in deep conversation. Papo also got a visit from the federal agent and wanted to get Nutsy's take on it. "Yeah, he popped in Sista one night too. This doesn't concern us," Nutsy says.

"Well, now that the kid, Donolla, and that asshole from the city are all cooked, it's bringing attention to Four Square that we don't need."

"What asshole?"

"You didn't hear? That pistol swindling degenerate from the city got strangled."

"Who ya talkin' about?"

"Big Charlie. They found him at some abandoned site with strap marks across his throat."

"Well, that has nothin' to do with us."

"Yeah well, everyone thinks it was Leo. If it's true, he's gotta be taken care of before he –"

Nutsy pauses and asks, "How many times I gotta say it? I'm not gettin' involved."

They catch eyes for a moment and then Papo replies, "Alright… on a different note. We priced out the turf and it's much more than we thought."

"How much?"

"One and a half times."

"Do we have anyone on the inside?"

"Nutsy, this ain't the kind of shit that falls off a truck."

"How about we carve out the bases with dirt, like a real field? That should help a little."

"Yeah, it will probably look nicer anyway… and the gravel. We should probably go ten inches instead of eight."

"Well, that we can get from Trillo, right?"

"I'll see. He owes me a favor."

"He still owes me money too."

"Will you eat it?"

"Only, if he gives it to us for cost."

Later that night, Nutsy sits at the island in his kitchen and makes a call on his cell phone. His mother, Carmela, answers her phone while sitting on her lanai in Delray Beach, Florida. "Well, I guess your fingers aren't broken after all," she sarcastically says.

Nutsy laughs and replies, "Yeah, they all still work, ma."

"It's been over a week since I called, Nuccio. No phone call, no nothing. You know, I could be in the hospital and you'd never even know it."

"I'm sorry. I've been busy."

"You should never be too busy for your mother."

"You're right… how's the pinochle games going?"

"Never mind the pinochle… what's this I hear?"

"I don't know. Wudya hear?"

"You might have some issues with your heart now."

"Nah, just a little agita and stress. I'm changing my ways anyway."

"Changing your ways? What does that even mean?"

"My lifestyle. I gave up drinking and cursing."

"Don't be a wise ass with me. You better go back to the doctor."

Nutsy laughs and replies, "How'd ya find out anyhow?"

"From the same birdy that you always seem to hear everything from."

Sammy has finally been moving around better with her ankle and slowly getting back to her ways. She has been spending more time with Bono after school and on the weekends. She even joined in a few karate classes that Bono has still been taking from time to time.

The lady instructor loves working out with Sammy since Sammy's a natural powerhouse. The instructor has been taking it slowly with Sammy because of her ankle.

It's an unseasonably warm day and Sammy and Bono sit in a neighborhood park to get some fresh air after one of their karate lessons. They are wondering how their relationship would wind up since they are both graduating this year from high school and have plans to join the military.

At this point, neither one has sent back their application since they have both been waiting to see what the other one does first. Nothing has been mentioned about it for a while until now since the deadline is approaching soon. "Do you still plan on going into the army?" Sammy asks.

"I would like to but…"

"But what?"

"I might have to go back down South."

"Why?" This is a total surprise to Sammy.

"My father's not doing well."

"Isn't your mother with him?"

"No, they divorced a long time ago. He has some rare blood disease."

"Oh, I'm really sorry to hear that. Can he come up here?" Sammy figures this might keep Bono around.

"My father and uncle never got along."

Leo never moved out of Squalo's apartment and is still around annoying him to no end. He had told his father another apartment deal was reneged on by the owner and he is still searching for another one to move into.

Their relationship has been heading downhill quickly and Squalo is starting to feel nervous about the federal agent who has been poking around. Squalo is not thrilled with Leo's current behavior anyway. He knows Leo is like a loose cannon just waiting to explode.

Squalo is torn since he's trying his hardest to keep peace with his son, but also doesn't want to get dragged into anymore situations because of his son's irrational behavior. He heard through the grapevine about Big Charlie getting strangled and wonders if his son is responsible for it. Leo totally denies it though.

Squalo's figuring that Leo is becoming desperate and needs to make moves, and quickly. He has been toying with the idea of lending Leo money so maybe that might take some pressure off Leo's mind for the time being.

FOUR SQUARE MILES, *the final project*

At this point, Squalo has no idea that Leo owes Detective Dons a large amount of cash for assisting him with the hit on Ladro's brother during the botched robbery.

While sitting on the couch, Leo is on the phone with the claim investigator and says, "I wasn't around when that check got sent out, so I didn't know my sister already mailed it."

The rep relies, "This is a long time for a check to get lost, sir."

"You can talk to the post office about that. I have nothing to do with it."

"But you said your father gave the agent cash. So, I'm a little confused by all this."

"My father hasn't been remembering things too well lately. I think his age is catching up to him."

Squalo wanders by and gives Leo an annoyed look.

"Well, I'll show it to my manager again and let you know what she says."

Leo becomes short and replies, "You said that bullshit already. I'm losing tons of business now. Just get it approved!" Leo hangs up the call.

Squalo says from the kitchen, "His age is catching up to him. What kind of shit is that?"

"This fucking rep is pulling my chain now."

"Yeah whatever… I'm getting tired of being tangled up in your bullshit anyway."

There is a knock on the door and Leo asks, "Don't tell me it's that fucking agent again?"

"I wouldn't doubt it," Squalo replies while heading toward the door. He peeks through the peep hole and notices a stunning looking woman standing in the hallway. "Can I help you?" Squalo asks.

"Yes, I'm looking for Leonardo DeSanto. I understand he might be staying here."

Squalo hesitates since he has never seen this striking woman before. "Well, is he here?" she asks again.

Squalo opens the door and says, "I'm sorry, but he ain't using my apartment to get his rocks off anymore."

"Excuse me."

"You heard me."

The woman holds up her federal badge and says, "You must have me mistaken for someone else… I'm Agent O'Leary and I'm taking over my partner's cases."

Squalo just stares since he stuck his foot in his mouth and then tries to play it off, "Where is he, Florida collecting his pension?"

"Quite the opposite. He had a heart attack, so he's on leave. I'll be taking over from here… have you seen him or not?" Agent O'Leary was assigned the prior federal agent's cases and wants to make her presence known.

Squalo was getting ready to answer when Leo appears behind him. "Yeah, I'm Leo. What can I do for you?"

At first, they both notice how attractive each other is, but Agent O'Leary quickly gets down to business. "Is there a better place to talk? I need to ask a few questions."

"I think he already told you, this is his place, not mine," Leo replies.

Squalo opens the door to let Agent O'Leary in. "We can at least talk in the foyer like adults," Squalo says while his heart begins to race. He knows his son can't help himself around attractive women.

Agent O'Leary steps into the foyer and peeks around. "Nice place. I gotta say."

"What's your name again?" Leo asks.

"I'm Agent O'Leary."

"You look much better than the last jerkoff that came by."

"I'm glad you approve." They stare for a moment.

Squalo cuts in. He knows his son is still annoyed from his phone call with the claims rep and loves creating tension. Besides, he can tell Leo is now eyeing Agent O'Leary. "Alright, can we get this over with? I need to be somewhere in a half an hour."

Leo looks Agent O'Leary up and down. He can't believe how stunning she is while a few dirty thoughts flow through his mind. O'Leary catches him peeking down toward her firm thighs and asks, "You like them?"

Leo is caught off guard and asks, "Like what?"

"My legs. You've been staring at them since I walked in."

"Actually, they ain't bad at all. Nice and tight, the way I like them."

Squalo becomes annoyed and barks out, "Let's get this done already. I got an important meeting and don't have time for bullshit talk."

Agent O'Leary gets straight to business and whips out the photo of Leo, Miguel, and Big Charlie since she feels she needs to get to the point. "Does this photo look familiar to you?"

Leo takes a glimpse and replies, "No, not really. What are you guys following me around now?"

"Well, let me refresh your memory. This photo was taken the same day Charles Niko was found in the bushes strangled to death."

"I don't know a Charles Niko."

"Well, maybe you know him as Big Charlie."

Squalo's eyes open wide, and Agent O'Leary notices his reaction. "You know him?"

Squalo replies, "Who doesn't know that degenerate?"

"Apparently, your son doesn't. Which I find very hard to believe."

"Well, I knew him as Little Charlie. I've been away for a while so maybe he grew up."

"What were you doing down there that day?"

"Going for a walk."

"A walk down there?"

"Yeah why, is that a crime?"

"Just so you know, Miguel doesn't seem as convincing as you do. Hopefully, he doesn't crack first. Thank you for your time." Agent O'Leary opens the door and walks out.

Squalo glares at Leo with an irate look. He feels Leo has something to do with Big Charlie's incident. Leo gives him a smirk and struts back into the living room.

CHAPTER 7

It's a decent day out and Nutsy, Ladro, Papo, and Paulie decide to get a quick nine holes in at Dun Woodie. The course is not too busy, so they are able to take their time to discuss business. Nutsy has always been a decent golfer, but Ladro is a hack and has been tearing up the course so far.

Nutsy and Ladro pull up to the third hole and step out of their cart. Papo and Paulie follow behind in their cart. "How do you guys play here? It's like I have to hit the ball to the right if I want it to go to the left," Ladro says.

Paulie laughs and replies, "You're right, Ladro. Way too many hills here."

Ladro replies, "I mean, this is insane. And I have geese shit all over my new shoes now."

Papo cuts in, "Will you two stop your complaining. We're out and it's a beautiful day… so, Nutsy, you've been quiet. Any word yet?"

Nutsy takes a warm-up swing on the tee. "This board is driving me nuts… still four to two last I heard, and the final vote is coming soon."

"That slime-ball inspector is in everyone's ear. You know that, right?" Papo replies.

Paulie says, "Forget this for now… have a beer and relax, Nutsy."

"I told ya guys, I stopped drinkin' and smokin' cigars."

Ladro takes a warm-up swing on the tee and accidentally tears up a chunk of grass that flies toward Paulie.

Paulie swats the chunk of grass away before hitting him in the face and says, "They're gonna have to reseed this whole course after you're done here."

"I fucking hate this game anyway. Just give me another beer," Ladro replies. He never had patience for golf.

Papo gets closer to Nutsy and whispers, "A new Fed paid me a visit the other day. How about you?"

Nutsy shakes his head no and takes another warm-up swing.

"I'm telling you, Nutsy. Leo's gonna take us all down with him."

Paulie overheard his brother's comment and says, "Look, I know you two always wanted to keep business in house, but if Nutsy doesn't get the sports park and that slime ball does, my family's coming in."

Papo gestures with his head for Nutsy to follow him. Nutsy follows Papo to an area at the side of the tee. "Did Detective Dons visit you?"

"Yeah, my house. Why?"

"He stopped by one of my towers. He's threatening to reopen our case again if we don't pull out."

"I'm tellin' ya right now. I'm not pullin' out of anything."

Nutsy and Ladro are now heading home after the round of golf. Nutsy told Ladro what Detective Dons said to Papo. Ladro is on board with Nutsy's decision to not pull out of the project yet. He also believes they are too close to the prize. Besides, nothing has been approved anyway.

Nutsy answers his buzzing cellphone, "What's up, Staci?"

Staci, their accountant, is in a meeting with the auditor discussing Sista's sales tax records and replies, "You got a minute, Nutsy?"

"Yeah, shoot."

"I'm in my office with the sales tax auditor. He's reneging on his offer."

"What does he want now?"

"Double."

"Tell him no way."

"Do you really want me to tell him that?"

"Ya said he's there?"

"Yeah, sitting by my desk."

"Tell him I'll be there in ten minutes." Nutsy hangs up.

Ladro asks, "What's wrong?"

"Would ya believe this auditor wants double now?"

"This state is going bust. They're nothing but a bunch of fucking thieves now."

Leo is sitting in the passenger seat of Miguel's Cadi heading toward Leo's shop. Squalo told Leo he is not driving him around anymore since he is concerned about how things are progressing. So, Leo has now been pestering Miguel for rides.

They pull up in front of the shop and the claim adjuster steps out of his car. Leo says to Miguel, "Wait here. Let me straighten this guy out."

Leo and the adjuster meet up in front of the rubble and the adjuster says, "Personally, I can't believe they're covering this after the policy lapsed."

"Hey, they received a post marked envelope, so what can I say?"

The adjuster believes there is something fishy about this claim but cannot say otherwise since the insurance company is honoring it. So, he goes forward scanning the grounds to prepare an estimate. After Leo and the adjuster roam through the damage, Leo gets back into Miguel's car. "I gotta stop by my sister's job," Leo says.

"Where?"

"1st Street. The Vernon Bank."

Miguel nods and remains quiet. He is currently wondering if the incident with Big Charlie could somehow come back to him. Although he didn't knock off Big Charlie, he witnessed the incident which makes him an accessory for not reporting it to authorities.

Miguel has been quiet during their car ride and Leo senses something is not right with him. Agent O'Leary has been pestering Miguel also, and he is wavering with making a deal with her. He cannot see any other way out of this predicament.

"Did you get a visit from a fed lately?" Leo nonchalantly asks but already knows the answer considering Agent O'Leary's comment to him.

"No, not yet. Did you?" Miguel doesn't want Leo to know he already received a visit. He feels Leo would not be comfortable with knowing he had, and Miguel is starting to not trust Leo's judgment anymore. He knows Leo could take care of business if need be, but it's his irrational behavior that is troubling Miguel.

"The other day. Some smoking hot agent banged on my father's door. I couldn't keep my eyes off her."

"Lucky you. No one came to me so far."

"That's strange. Because she mentioned your name."

"Why would she mention my name?"

"How about you tell me why?"

"I have no clue." Miguel pulls over in front of the bank.

"I'll be right back," Leo replies and opens the door.

Miguel nods while Leo steps out of the car and then heads toward the bank. Miguel gazes out the driver's side window. He is watching pedestrians stroll across a bridge that loops over railroad tracks while toying with the idea of telling Leo he cannot be involved with his project anymore.

Leo struts into the bank and takes a seat in front of Belinda's desk. Blackie glances out the window of her office and shakes her head. Leo continuously stopping in the bank is getting on her nerves.

Belinda starts off the conversation. "Your mortgage will never be approved until the claim is settled."

"It's done. I just met with the adjuster."

"They approved it?"

"With the September postmark, they had no choice."

"How did you get it postmarked?"

"Let's just say, I'm slowly getting favors returned to me."

Belinda slides a stack of papers toward Leo and says, "Here, have fun."

"I thought you were filling these out?"

"No, you can."

"Isn't that your job now?"

Belinda just stares and remains quiet.

"Fine, I'll get Maria to do it then." Leo snatches the papers off Belinda's desk, stands up, and heads into Blackie's office.

Blackie just stares at Leo with an annoyed look.

Leo places the stack of papers onto her desk and says, "I need you to fill these out. It's for my shop."

"Do me a favor. Take your papers and get the fuck out of my office."

"Wow, I'm sure your manager would love to hear how you're treating a customer."

"I am the manager, idiot."

"You have my money yet?"

"Yeah, go three blocks west, two blocks east, and it's sitting under a pile of dog shit," Blackie sarcastically replies.

Leo gathers up the papers then heads back out. He passes by Belinda again and says, "I'll be back when they're finished."

Leo continues and struts out of the bank. Belinda enters Blackie's office and says, "I'm really sorry about this. I'll tell him he can't come in anymore if you want me to."

"We can't. He hasn't done anything wrong yet."

The next morning, Nutsy is at the abandoned site standing by the same rusty fence he usually does, and gazes toward the field. The field has turned into nothing but weeds and unkempt dirt. It is disheartening in a way, but he's currently envisioning his proposal.

A large baseball field will be in the middle of the park with smaller fields scattered around the grounds. Built into

FOUR SQUARE MILES, *the final project*

the stands, will be an announcer's booth and an area for college coaches to scout out players. Nutsy's even hoping professional scouts will visit the complex.

Nutsy's picturing this park to be self-contained and give the players an experience of a lifetime. On the far-left side, two buildings will occupy the area, but will be contained for safety reasons. One building will be a home for special needs children and the other a school. The school will be self-sufficient so it could take in commuters for a yearly fee.

Nutsy's vision is clear as day. He can envision it all right in front of him at this very moment. He just needs the final approval from the board now.

Papo currently has The Quad together in his Venetian style decorated apartment. They are discussing Nutsy's project in his dining room. This project is something neither of them have ever gotten involved with before and is unsettling. The project will cost millions with the hope it could attract families that are willing to pay for their children to play baseball.

Although they all love the concept behind it, this is business and not to be taken lightly. Gloria is one hundred percent on board since her involvement with Billy has taken off to a new level. They have been spending a lot of time together but keeping it as quiet as possible. She is loaded anyway, so to her the money is no object.

Gloria lives in a different town and Billy has been spending most of his time at her place. Her house and estate like property is relaxing to him and he's been enjoying some peace and quiet.

Tiffany, one of the elite members of The Quad, a real money contributor, has access to billions through her hedge fund contacts. Plus, she is the sister of Marcus and Staci, Nutsy's lawyer and accountant.

Tiffany loves the idea of developing the park but is not certain of her investment toward it. She usually invests in towers and office complexes like what Papo deals with, since they are easier to gage a profit from. This sports complex has everyone puzzled on how it could truly sustain itself.

Although Nutsy has reassured everyone that parents would have no issue paying for their children to play ball, this is a concept The Quad is not experienced with. The only reason why The Quad is considering it, is because of Nutsy, and the fact that Papo would be the general contractor of the project.

Papo knows how to manipulate the subs and suppliers to keep the cost down. The only issue is the suppliers would be different than who he regularly deals with for this project.

The board is still torn with Nutsy's proposal. So far two board members are one hundred percent for it and four are against it, one being the inspector who is continuously pushing Miguel's condo project.

The inspector has been in everyone's ear trying his hardest to get them to knock Nutsy's proposal down. Billy is working his angle behind the scenes to get the majority vote or at least make it even. He also knows this inspector is working behind the scenes against Nutsy. If Billy could sway one

FOUR SQUARE MILES, *the final project* 81

more board member and make it an even vote, he knows the deciding factor lies with the mayor.

He currently has the approval of the retired schoolteacher and another lady who is a local business owner. Billy knows he does not have a shot with the inspector and two of his associates. But there is one that he feels he can still sway.

CHAPTER 8

Lately, Leo has been roaming around by bus, train, and foot attempting to rebuild his illegal enterprise. Leo is currently in the back seat of Detective Dons' car. Dons is fed up with waiting for his money and is now threatening Leo for payment. "Let me make this very clear. You either have my money by next week, or I'll peg you for the kid in the woods and Ladro's brother."

"That's bullshit. You did Ladro's brother, not me."

"Let me say this again… next week or you're done."

"You know something, everyone forgets. The shit I did for you years back should be payment in full."

"What have you done for me lately? Remember that saying?"

Leo just puckers his lips.

"One week or the report gets filed."

Leo gazes out the window. He knows there is a slim chance of getting that type of money in a week. Plus, he cannot take the chance with showing the police the bullet in case Blackie was telling him the truth about it coming from one of his illegal guns. "I'm close to getting my loan approved for my shop. I just need a few more weeks." Leo is trying to buy more time.

"What loan?"

"I'm financing it."

"You've been away too long, Sonny Boy. These banks take forever to get approvals today. Besides, you got nothing to show. No income, no assets. You're like a dead mule on paper."

Leo knows Dons is probably right and is starting to feel a bit anxious. His eyes twitch a little. Once Leo's eyes start twitching, anything could happen next. He slowly reaches into his jacket pocket and throws out a threat, "Well, you're gonna wait."

"Next week, or you'll be spending the rest of your life staring at a cement wall… now get the fuck out of my car!"

Leo opens the back door and slides out. He pauses by the driver's side door and Detective Dons says, "And don't ever tell me I'm gonna wait again."

"You're right. You're not." Leo yanks out a pistol from his jacket pocket and pumps a few rounds into Detective Dons' chest. Dons gasps for air while anxiously drawing his pistol.

Leo fires two more rounds hitting the side of his head. Detective Dons hunches over the steering wheel and is clearly finished. Leo bolts away down the street on foot. It's dark out so a few residents who had heard the shots can't quite make Leo out.

It's a half an hour later and police cars are scattered around Detective Dons' car with their red lights blaring through the darkness. Agent O'Leary just arrived at the scene. For many years, the detectives in Four Square operated on their own, but the increasing violent activity in this city is alarming to the feds and they now plan to become more involved in the local cases.

Agent O'Leary stands by Detective Dons' driver's side window and turns her head. It is not a pleasant scene, at all. "So, what do we have here?" she asks a police officer.

The police officer replies, "It looks like a close-range hit."

"Any idea who this guy is?"

"Yeah, a city detective."

"Clean or dirty?"

The police officer remains silent. He knows damn well Detective Dons was as corrupt as they come but does not want to admit it since he's not exactly sure who he's speaking with.

Agent O'Leary notices his hesitation and she becomes a little more forceful. Although she has stunning looks and appears more like a model, she knows how to be curt if need be. "Are you hard of hearing? I asked you if he's clean or dirty?"

The police officer replies, "I barely knew the guy." He is not ready to admit the truth.

Agent O'Leary has heard that Four Square is a complex city to work cases in. It's very difficult at times to determine who is clean or dirty in this city and not many people talk. So, she wants to make sure her presence is known around here. "Take a walk with me."

Agent O'Leary walks off to the side of the road. The officer reluctantly follows her. "Okay, I need you to do me a favor. You make sure everyone knows I'm around and if I ask a question, I'll expect an answer. If I don't receive cooperation, I'm gonna make their life miserable. Do you understand where I'm coming from?"

The officer knows very well this is a threat and nods yes.

Agent O'Leary asks, "He was dirty, or you understand, or both?"

The officer hesitantly replies, "Both."

"Who oversees this city?"

"I'm not sure what you mean."

"You know, the streets. Who has the most influence around here?"

"Probably Nutsy."

"The bookmaker I hear about?"

The police officer nods yes.

"Thank you for your cooperation." Agent O'Leary smiles and heads toward the other side of the car.

Belinda is sitting in Blackie's office discussing Leo and what he is up to. Blackie doesn't like the idea of Belinda helping him out with a mortgage loan, but she feels they cannot be the ones to deny him. They are required to at least take the application and send it to the main office for the bank's underwriters to review.

Munchie strolls into the bank and notices the two of them in Blackie's office. He knocks on the door and Blackie opens it. "Hey, Doc."

Belinda gives Munchie a peck on the lips. "We're going out for dinner later, right?" Munchie asks.

"If you're still up to it."

"Hey, I heard Scottie's has a new chef and she's great," Blackie says.

"Seems like a good choice to me," Munchie replies.

Belinda asks, "Did you come in to say hello, or do you need something?"

"Both… I need to make a withdrawal."

"I can do it. How much?" Blackie asks.

"Five thousand."

Blackie says, "That's an expensive dinner."

Munchie replies, "I wish. Most of it is going to your brother."

Belinda says, "You've been losing a lot lately. You better start taking it easy."

"It was just that one field goal that killed me."

Belinda replies, "One field goal this week. A fumble last week. An interception the week before that."

"I know. I know."

Blackie hands Munchie a slip and says, "Here, fill it out. I'll get it for you."

Munchie fills out the withdrawal slip and hands it back to Blackie. "I'll be right back." Blackie walks out.

Belinda says, "Seriously, you need to start slowing down. It's becoming too much now."

"Well, the money Nutsy gave me back is like found money anyway."

"That's not found money. He gave it back because you helped him out."

"Still. He didn't have to."

"Just slow it down."

Munchie nods. He has no intention of stopping. In fact, he couldn't if he tried to. He's addicted and knows it.

After getting the cash together, Blackie enters her office with an envelope and says, "This is some stack you're giving my brother."

Munchie just nods while slipping the envelope into his pocket. Feeling how thick the envelope is, makes Munchie really realize how much money is stuffed in it.

"Okay, I'll see you later," Belinda says and then pecks him on the lips.

Munchie smiles and walks out.

Blackie says, "I don't understand why he gambles so much. I mean, he's a doctor and makes good income. What does he need this for?"

"I don't get it either. But I can tell it's becoming a problem. Between you and me, when he loses big, he can't get it up that night."

"Are you kidding me?"

"No, thank God he's a doctor. At least he can take one of those blue pills."

"Do they work?"

"Work? It's like dynamite when he takes one."

Blackie laughs and says, "Alright, let's get back to your brother and figure out what to say to the underwriters."

Belinda replies, "I'll say whatever is needed for them to turn him down."

Nutsy had to meet with the sales tax auditor again at Staci's office. When they had first met, it ended in an argument, so Staci asked for another meeting. The auditor was pushing for double in sales receipts and Nutsy told him no way. He does make more than what he says but not double, so Nutsy had no problem pushing back.

After Nutsy had thrown the auditor a few insults that created a bit of tension in the room, Staci calmed everyone down. They all finally agreed on a small increase from the earlier figure, but it wasn't that large of an increase for Nutsy to be concerned with. He still makes much more than the agreed upon figure.

After the auditor left Staci's office, Nutsy and Staci consulted about his project and how the income and expenses would work. They decided that the best avenue would be a non-profit structure for the home and school. The park itself would be structured as an LLC corporation with Nutsy's family trust being the majority shareholder.

Although Nutsy is not an educated person on paper, all the research he has done on his own regarding corporate and trust set-up ideas allows him to have an intelligent conversation with Staci. He still insists that he does not want to appear on any of the documents that has Staci puzzled. She decides to not press Nutsy on this matter since he has already mentioned it a few times.

Nutsy was always the type of person who needed to research ideas and items of interest to him. It started with his passion for numbers at a younger age when he spent many nights by himself practicing addition and subtraction tables.

Nutsy can be obsessive when it comes to things he loves. Many people do not see this in him since he keeps his interests private. Kathy knows very well how Nutsy is and feels this sports complex will eventually consume all his time. Not that he would purposely ignore his family, but the burning desire to complete a task, whatever it may be, consumes his thoughts and energy.

In some respects, he is a perfectionist on the inside, but still a tough street-smart man on the outside. Kathy can tell this obsession is starting to happen since N-J's situation seems to be put on the back burner by Nutsy.

Kathy had all intentions of leaving her job to care for N-J on a full time basis. She felt this was needed for their family and her son's wellbeing since they now know N-J's true feelings.

But there are two issues delaying this. The sports park that Nutsy is slowly becoming consumed with and the fact that Kathy carries the health benefits from her job.

She is worried that Nutsy may need some sort of procedure because of his condition and is concerned about giving up the benefits. She is also becoming annoyed because Nutsy keeps minimizing his chest pain and disregards his medical appointments.

Kathy had a talk with N-J about their plan being delayed because of Nutsy's condition, but N-J thought it was just an excuse. He always had a special relationship with his mother and was really looking forward to staying home for good. He now thinks this will never happen.

Nutsy and Billy meet up at Joey's Pizzeria to discuss the project, and of course, have a slice of their Sicilian pie. Nutsy and Billy have not spent as much time together lately since

FOUR SQUARE MILES, *the final project*

Billy's relationship with Gloria has been taking off. Billy reassured Nutsy that he is still pushing for the project behind the scenes.

Nutsy's been quiet and Billy senses something is off with him. "If the project is too much, let me know."

Nutsy takes a bite of his Sicilian slice and replies, "It's not that, Billy. I got an issue with N-J now."

"What issue?"

"He knows he has to stay there a little longer."

"Why? I thought you and Kathy decided she'll stay home with him?"

"She's afraid to leave her job right now."

"How come? It's not like they pay her that much."

"It's because of me."

"Don't tell me you changed your mind?"

"No, I didn't... I might need a procedure done."

"What kind of procedure?"

Nutsy hesitantly replies, "For my heart."

"Jesus Christ! I should've been told this immediately... wait until I see her."

"I told her not to tell you. I wanted to."

"That's it. I'm calling off the project."

"No way!"

"This is your life we're talking about here. What's the prognosis?"

"I don't know yet."

"Why not?"

"I've been holdin' off gettin' the tests done."

Billy was never convinced that Nutsy's project was solid in the first place. He cannot grasp the travel baseball concept and now with this news, Billy's totally against it. "I'll tell you what. You either get checked out, or I'm killing the project. I don't need my son-in-law in a box because he was too stubborn to get help."

"It has nothin' to do with that."

"Oh yeah, then what?" Billy is now annoyed.

"I can't say. Trust me on this."

"Sure, that's an easy answer, isn't it?"

"It's never easy, Billy, believe me."

Nutsy and Billy catch eyes. Billy can sense something is going through Nutsy's mind.

CHAPTER 9

Agent O'Leary is now in Sista asking a waitress if Nuccio Gento is around. By asking for Nutsy by his formal name, the waitress thought it was important, so she looked to see if Nutsy was in The Headquarters. No one from this city walks in here and asks for Nutsy by his formal name.

He wasn't in The Headquarters, so the waitress went back downstairs to let Agent O'Leary know. O'Leary hands the waitress a business card while Nutsy now strolls in after finishing his conversation with Billy. Nutsy has never seen this attractive woman before and catches eyes with her. "Oh, here he is," the waitress says.

Nutsy pauses by the two of them and asks, "Can I help ya?"

Agent O'Leary replies, "You just might be able to. I'm investigating a few cases around here and would like to ask you a few questions."

"Are ya a new city detective? Because I've never seen ya before," Nutsy asks.

"No, I work for the Federal Bureau. Do you have a minute?"

Nutsy nods and guides her toward a quiet table in the back of the bar. She has an athletic shape like Blackie, but darker in complexion. They both take a seat and Nutsy asks, "Can I offer ya anything? Coffee? A muffin?"

"I'm fine. Thank you… I understand you oversee the streets around here."

"I don't oversee a thing. I'm just a business owner who's tryin' to make ends meet."

"You seem like a serious man, so let me be blunt with you. I don't like games. I don't like criminals, and I surely don't like guys who think I'm a fool."

Nutsy smiles and replies, "Well, I guess you'll like me because I don't apply to any of them."

They stare at one another. Nutsy can't believe how striking she is for an agent. He thinks she could be an actress or even a model for that matter.

Agent O'Leary on the other hand, knows she is sitting across from a savvy city guy who has survived these tough streets for years with hardly any blemishes on his record. He might have a few scars here and there, but nothing serious to speak of.

The waitress approaches the table and asks, "Can I get either of you anything?"

Agent O'Leary replies, "A glass of water would be great."

The waitress nods at Nutsy and he says, "I'll have a coffee and an apple turnover."

The waitress nods and heads toward the kitchen.

O'Leary is ready to get down to business. "We're looking to nab Leonardo again. We believe he's the cause for the increase in violence around here."

"Then grab him."

"It's not that simple. He knows how to move in and out without any traces." Agent O'Leary is not certain Leo is the person causing the issues, so she is also sizing up Nutsy. Nutsy is not a fool and knows this to be the case. He has been down this road before.

"You guys are the ones who let him out with that ridiculous new law the state just passed, not me."

"Believe me, I wasn't crazy about it either. Do you know how many guys I put away that are back on the street?"

"Yeah, I'm sure."

Sammy happens to be looking for her father and spots him sitting in the back of the tavern. At first, she wonders why he is sitting with this beautiful woman but then recognizes her as she gets closer. "Sensei O'Leary, what a surprise," Sammy says with a smile.

Agent O'Leary stands up and gives Sammy a hug. "Samantha, what brings you here?"

Nutsy cuts in, "Wait, you two know each other?"

"I take karate lessons from Sensei," Sammy replies.

"Karate lessons? Since when?"

"Well, they're really for Bono, but Sensei lets me join in." Agent O'Leary happens to be the karate instructor that Bono originally went to.

Nutsy glances away. This is the last thing he needs, his daughter and the Federal Agent who is questioning him to be on a friendly basis.

"Please, let me not interrupt you two," Agent O'Leary says.

"I just need a hundred dollars for my gown deposit. It's due today."

"Just a hundred, ha?" Nutsy sarcastically replies while whipping out a stack of bills from his pants pocket.

"Don't worry, I'll need more shortly."

"That, I already know."

Agent O'Leary's eyes open wide. She can't believe how thick the stack is. Nutsy hands off a hundred-dollar bill to Sammy and says, "Here, now let us finish our conversation."

Sammy gives Agent O'Leary a quick hug and says, "I can't wait to train again. You're a great instructor." Sammy pecks Nutsy on the cheek and says, "Thank you, dad." Sammy walks away.

Nutsy asks, "I take it you're also a martial arts instructor?"

"For years… I love teaching young ladies like your daughter. She has tremendous potential."

"Yeah great… let's finish this. I gotta meeting soon." Nutsy is somewhat annoyed now and Agent O'Leary can sense it.

"I think it's great she wants to become a Navy Seal. It's a tough road but a nice dream."

"Yeah, I'm sure ya do... are ya here for her or me?" Nutsy is becoming short now with his answers.

"We want him back off the streets. Period."

"That's your job, not mine."

"You have just as much to gain."

"Oh yeah? And how is that?"

"We have information he's looking to make a run at this city, brick by brick. If that's true, you better get used to seeing Feds all over these streets... and... you can kiss that sports park goodbye."

"How do ya know about that?"

"Your daughter mentioned how excited you are about it... I do have to admit, I think it's a great thing if you can pull it off."

"I appreciate your nod of approval, but I asked ya how ya know about Leo?"

"Intelligence."

"Well, I'm not sure how intelligent your intelligence is."

"I was hoping to not have to take this route, but I can tell you're not going to make this easy." O'Leary slides a piece of paper out from her jacket pocket and reads aloud, "Two local young men plead not guilty to a shootout with notorious downtown group."

"That was all hearsay."

"I don't think they gave you enough credit… there didn't seem to be a shootout based on the file. It looked more like an ambush."

Nutsy has a feeling where this conversation is heading and becomes defensive. "I've already been cleared, so your reasoning means nothin' right now."

"You were only cleared because this city swept it under the rug and rightly so. This was a bad group that got what they deserved."

"I thought ya didn't like games? Ya seem to be playin' 'em with me right now."

"You're right so let me get straight to the point. You help me nail this guy and I'll make sure your file doesn't land on my supervisor's desk. And just to be clear, that would be on a Federal level, not city."

The Mayor is in her office with the schoolteacher. They are discussing Nutsy's project and are trying to figure out how they could get one more vote to help push it through.

So far, it's still four to two in Miguel's favor. If they could get the last member to change their mind, the approval would be guaranteed with the mayor being the deciding factor. Right now, the last member is swaying on the fence.

The plumber's wife heads into Sista to look for Nutsy. She used up all the money he had given her at the cemetery and decided to take him up on his offer to stop by if she needed more.

A waitress heads upstairs with her since she knows Nutsy is in The Headquarters. The waitress bangs on the door and waits. Ladro answers the door and asks, "What's up?"

"She wants to talk to Nutsy."

"Hold on one minute."

Ladro heads over toward the bar were Nutsy is counting stacks of cash and says, "I think the plumber's wife is here to see you. What do you want me to tell her?"

Nutsy places the stacks of cash under the counter behind the bar and says, "Send her in."

Ladro walks back toward the door and says, "Come in."

The plumber's wife thanks the waitress and walks in. At first, she is a bit nervous seeing all the people roaming around, but then notices Nutsy by the bar. She heads over and Nutsy asks, "How's your daughter?"

"I guess okay... I hate to ask but you told me to stop in if I needed more money."

"Yeah, I know. Hold on one second." Nutsy presses Presto's number on his phone and waits for him to answer.

Presto is currently soft tossing baseballs to his son in his basement and pauses when he hears his phone buzzing.

He notices Nuccio on the display and answers, "How did the proposal go?"

"I think okay. Thanks again for all your help and the recommendations."

"Hey listen, we're all in this together. I would love to see that park developed just as much as you do. So, what's up?"

"Remember that lady I asked ya about?"

"The one whose husband had the car accident?"

"Yeah. She's here right now. Can you talk to her?"

Presto gestures to his son, wait one minute, and his son rolls his eyes. "Yeah, put her on."

Nutsy hands the phone to the lady and says, "It's an old friend in the insurance business. See if he can help you out."

"Hi, this is Patty. I appreciate you taking the time to speak with me."

Presto replies, "Well, hopefully I can help. And my condolences for your husband."

"Thank you."

"So, tell me what happened?"

"Well, my husband applied for life insurance and unfortunately had the accident before he took the exam for it."

"Did they send you a letter?"

"Yes, it said the application wasn't approved because all the requirements weren't completed and, once they are, they'll reconsider."

"Did he pay anything with the application?"

"Yes, they sent the check back with the denial letter."

"Did they send the letter before or after the accident?"

"It was about two weeks after."

Michael shrugs at his father since he is becoming impatient and Presto gestures one more minute. "Alright, this is what I want you to do. Call the company and tell them what you just told me. I think he might still be covered."

"How?"

"Most binders cover accidents whether the exam was completed or not."

"Oh my God! That would be great. Thank you so much."

"I hope it works out."

Patty hands the phone back to Nutsy and says, "Thank you so much."

"I didn't do anything."

"You did more than you know." She walks out and forgets to take what she originally came for, more money.

Nutsy continues the conversation with Presto, "What did ya say? She's doing cartwheels out of here."

"She might have a shot, Nuccio."

"Is there anyone we can pay off to push this through?"

Presto laughs and replies, "It doesn't work that way in this business."

"Ya just haven't gotten to the right person. Thanks for your help, I gotta go." Nutsy hangs up the call.

Agent O'Leary stops into Miguel's office to discuss the photo with him once again. Based on the notes from the prior agent, she feels Miguel knows more than he says he does. She is pressing him like she did with Nutsy, only harder.

Miguel guides her into his conference room and they both take a seat around a table. "Just so you know, I had a nice discussion with Nutsy."

"Yeah, so?"

"He might be willing to help out."

"No fucking way. Nutsy doesn't talk to law enforcement."

"Hey, people change."

"You keep on stopping by and I keep telling you I have nothing for you."

"You're afraid of this guy, aren't you?"

"I didn't get to where I am by being afraid of anyone."

"You can feel it, can't you?"

"Feel what?"

"The walls closing in on you. This room is getting tighter by the day and you know it."

"Whatever."

"Take about half of this room and that will be your new home for a long time unless you start talking."

It's about two hours later and Agent O'Leary now bangs on Squalo's door again. Squalo peeks through the peephole and mumbles, "This fucking lady again?"

"I heard that," Agent O'Leary replies from the hallway.

Squalo opens the door and says, "Good, you were supposed to. What now?"

"Your son here?"

"No."

"Where is he?"

"I stopped keeping tabs on him after he went to jail."

"Well, maybe you should again."

"What can I do for you? I'm busy."

"I'm taking over the case in Four Square regarding that kid who was dumped in the woods."

"Why are feds working that case? It was already assigned to a city detective."

"Because your son made it back out and people are slowly disappearing, that's why."

"Well, good luck. I know nothing about it." Squalo attempts to close the door but Agent O'Leary jams her foot in the doorway to prevent it from closing. "This is harassment, just so you know."

"Do you drive a white Cadi?"

"Yeah, so?"

"A late-night dog walker puts a Cadi at the same place that kid was dumped."

"I guess I own the only white Cadi in this state then."

"No, but I'm sure it might have remnants in it."

"You're fishing in a very large ocean right now, young lady."

"And I see you're not biting yet. But you will." Agent O'Leary heads down the hallway.

CHAPTER 10

Nutsy and Ladro stop into Curio's Deli on the main avenue of the city. You can tell it's an Italian Deli just by the smell of it. Christmas day is right around the corner, so the deli is busier than normal. Nutsy and Ladro head toward the back of the long line to place their orders.

Patty, the plumber's wife, strolls in with her daughter about ten minutes later. Her daughter is holding a small stuffed animal. Patty looks much different. She has a glow about her and cannot help but smile while noticing Nutsy in the store.

She hugs Nutsy tightly and says, "Thank you so much."

"For what?"

"Your friend was right. The binder covers accidents whether the exam was completed or not."

Nutsy smiles and says, "I'm glad it worked out."

"I'm so glad I ran into you that day at the cemetery."

"Yeah, me too."

The young girl looks at Nutsy and says, "You're like an angel that was sent to us by my daddy."

Nutsy rubs the top of her head and replies, "I think you're right."

Patty smiles and walks to the end of the line with her daughter while wiping a tear.

Nutsy and Ladro finally make it to the front of the line and Nutsy sarcastically says to the owner, "Shit, ya might need someone to walk ya to the bank."

The owner replies, "Ah, Nutsy, this is our time. It either makes or breaks the year… you want the regular order of antipasto you usually get?"

"Yeah, throw an extra half moon of the provolone in too. This guy eats it like he's Mickey."

The owner laughs and replies, "We can't get enough of that stuff. It sells like candy during Halloween." The owner looks at Ladro and asks, "How about you?"

"I'm going to his house, so he can buy the antipasto this year. That shit ain't cheap anymore."

"This year? It seems like I buy it every year. Who are you kidding?" Nutsy asks.

The owner laughs and asks, "Any cookies?"

Ladro replies, "Yeah, definitely. Throw in a few boxes with his order. They're assorted, right?"

"My order? What are ya comin' empty handed again?"

"I bring the homemade wine, don't I?"

A person behind them purposely coughs loudly.

"Oh, now it's your wine? I bought all the grapes, didn't I?"

"Do you know how much time it takes to make that?"

"Ya don't even do anythin' anymore. I give ya the pressed juice already. It's like having the tomatoes squashed before ya make the gravy."

A few more people behind them cough to hopefully speed things up. The owner nervously notices the line getting longer and longer while Nutsy and Ladro are going back and forth with each other.

Nutsy says, "Ya know… now that I'm thinkin' about it. Ladro's gonna pay ya this year."

"Why? You think I care? I'll pay right now. I don't give a shit. How much is it?"

"Everything? Cookies, cake, cheese, antipasto, and the meat pies?" the owner asks.

"Yeah, that's right. Everything. This guy thinks he's the only one that pays for anything around here." Ladro whips out his money from his pants pocket.

The owner replies, "Okay, it comes to two-hundred and seventy-five dollars."

"What? That's impossible. Recount it."

Nutsy laughs and says, "Now that I think about it, we always run short on the Gabagool and Struffoli. Throw more of that in too."

Ladro counts his stash.

Nutsy sarcastically says, "Two to one, he's short by a mile."

Kathy has been feeling the pressure all around lately. She knows her son is not happy one bit being back at the home. She's been trying to convince N-J that she needs to remain at her job in order to keep the health benefits that might be needed for his father.

N-J listens to her but does not completely buy her story. He believes everyone thinks he is different, and this is just a good excuse. He tries to convince his mother he would be good and stay home by himself, but his past incidences are not giving Kathy any comfort with that idea.

Kathy is currently sitting with N-J in the back room of the facility. She is trying her hardest to convince N-J that they all still love him. N-J just smiles and nods his head.

After she left the facility, Kathy gets into her car and just sits there for a moment. This was not a happy visit for her at all. She breaks down into tears and cannot help but think that her son is drifting away from her.

In a way, she is starting to become resentful of Nutsy. He has been prolonging seeing Munchie and seems to have only the sports park on his mind lately.

Kathy pulls away after wiping her tears with a napkin from her glove box and decides to call Blackie. Blackie is currently pulling up to her job and answers her phone. "It's early. Is everything all right?"

Kathy breaks down into tears again. She can't help herself. The pressure is becoming too unbearable.

"What's wrong?" Blackie asks.

"It's N-J. He's pulling away from me."

"Did you tell him it's only temporary?"

"Yeah… he doesn't want to hear it though."

"I don't know, Kathy. In a way you can't blame him."

"That's the problem. Especially, since we gave him a glimmer of hope."

"Come over later and we'll talk."

"Alright." Kathy hangs up the call and decides she is going to stop back home for a minute. She enters her house and sees Nutsy in the kitchen sipping his coffee at the island staring at plans for the complex. "Ya forget something?" Nutsy asks.

"No, I just came from N-J's."

"How's he doing?"

"Maybe if you stop staring at those plans all the time and visit him, you'll know."

"I do visit him."

"Yeah, when?"

"What's all the questions for?"

"You wanna know why? N-J is still there because of you."

"What are ya talkin' about?"

"You keep delaying seeing Munchie."

Nutsy just stares since he knows he has been. Kathy continues, "I'm giving you until the end of next month to see Munchie, then I'm putting my papers in."

"We'll have no coverage then. What happens if I need it?"

"You can pay Cobra then."

"Cobra? That's like a few thousand a month."

"Well, it's either a few thousand for Cobra or a few thousand for your apartment… you decide."

Nutsy laughs and takes a sip of his coffee.

"Go ahead. Keep laughing like you always do. You lied to me and N-J."

"I didn't lie to anyone. Ya know this project is time consuming."

"You know something, Nutsy. I never thought I'd say this to you, but you're nothing but a hypocrite."

"Oh, now I'm a hypocrite?"

"That's right. You either get this done or start looking." Kathy walks out.

Nutsy sighs.

Blackie and Belinda are going over the day's events in Blackie's office while Leo struts in. He tosses a stack of papers onto Blackie's desk and says, "Here's the rest of the papers. This fucking bank better not ask for anything else."

Belinda arranges the papers and doesn't respond.

"Process it as fast as you can." Leo turns and struts out without waiting for a reply.

Blackie says, "Your brother is some piece of work."

"Yeah well." Belinda stands up and walks toward a garbage pail then chucks the papers into it. "Screw him. He never did anything for me."

"We have no choice but to send them up, Belinda."

"Let him go to another bank then."

Blackie starts picking the papers out of the garbage pail and replies, "Still, they have to be sent up."

"I thought coming here I'd finally get away from him. I should've known better."

"How do you think I feel?"

Nutsy is a little twisted after his conversation with Kathy regarding N-J and decides to have a meeting with some of his workers in The Headquarters. A few of them have fallen behind on their collections and their totals are mounting up.

Nutsy has been paying these guys their share of income out of his own pocket and he now wants all debts paid up.

"Alright, I'm making some changes around here. Your future pay is gonna be based on your collections."

One of the men replies, "That's not fair, Nutsy. It's not our problem people don't pay."

"Oh, no? Ya booked those bets, right?"

Ladro cuts in and says to the man, "We don't seem to have any issues collecting. Why do you?"

"Because we got all the deadbeats."

Nutsy replies, "It's because ya sit around all day staring at your phone… ya need to be in their faces constantly. Not texting smiley shit at them."

Ladro says to the man, "And stop mentioning the collections on social media, you moron."

"What's he doing?" Nutsy asks.

Ladro replies, "He can tell you."

The man replies, "I tell them how much they owe."

"Where, on the phone?" Nutsy asks.

The man nods and Nutsy says, "What do ya think you're a salesman now? Are ya nuts?"

"Nutsy, everyone communicates on social media now."

"Do me a favor. Stay off the phone and get on the street… this ain't Vegas."

"It's still not right."

"Not right!" Nutsy glances at an index card. "Here's your book. Tiny Tim owes two-grand. Mugzie owes three. Oh, this is great... Lenny the Lizard owes five. Five-grand while ya sit here and drink all my liquor."

"Nutsy, you know these guys are slow payers. Half of them don't even have jobs anymore."

"Then cut 'em off and find new players. I'm tired of babysitting you guys... ya know something, get out. All of you. And don't come back until ya have some cash."

The men stand up and head out, one by one.

Ladro asks, "Is that Agent busting your horns again?"

Nutsy nods and replies, "She's good, Ladro. She backed me into a corner real tight, like a clam."

After heading downstairs, Nutsy storms toward the exit and notices Agent O'Leary walking in again. He sighs while she approaches him. "We need to talk."

"What now?"

"Can we go somewhere private?"

Nutsy nods and guides Agent O'Leary toward the same table in the back where they had their discussion the last time. "Ya know, people are gonna start talkin' about us."

"Don't flatter yourself. You're not my type."

Nutsy peeks down at her hand and doesn't notice a ring on her finger. "Ya know, you look like that actress –"

"Halle?"

"Yup, that's right."

"I've heard that before… your daughter is cleared with the guy in the woods. But I gotta question you about someone else… what do you call this guy? Do… na—"

"Ya talkin' about Donnola?"

"Yeah, I guess so. What kind of names do you guys have around here?"

"Our names fit our personalities."

"What does Donnola mean?"

"It means weasel and that's just what he was."

"So, I guess you're Nutsy because you're nuts, ha?"

"I like walnuts, that's why."

"Yeah okay… the rumor is, you two didn't care for each other."

"Yeah, that's right. Since we were teenagers. It's no secret around here."

"Maybe you did the hit then."

Nutsy laughs and replies, "Yeah sure. I'm not an idiot."

"Then who else would've done this?"

"Agent O'Leary, if I wanted to be a crime solver, I would've gotten into law enforcement."

"I gotta admit, Nuccio. You're a little different."

"Yeah, and why's that?"

"You're a criminal, but likable in a strange way."

"I told ya before, I'm not a criminal. I'm a business owner."

"It's too bad. Most of these guys are total morons, you're not. It's gonna be a waste of talent if I have to take you down."

"My talent has only kept me alive."

"I would say lucky is more like it."

"I don't believe in luck. We all make our own beds, don't we?"

It's about 5:30pm and Leo just finished fooling around with another woman in his bedroom. Squalo wanders into the apartment and notices this woman heading out of the bedroom with Leo while reapplying her lipstick.

Squalo doesn't acknowledge either one of them, then heads into his bedroom to get changed. Leo walks the woman to the door and says, "Don't worry about him."

She nods and heads out. Leo closes the door and turns to see Squalo standing behind him with a pissed-off look. "Don't creep up on me like this. Unless you want your head in the wall."

"Didn't I say, I don't want anyone in my apartment?" Squalo barks out.

"Hey, I have a lot of catching up to do."

"I'm not screwing around anymore, Leo. And did you call O'Leary back?"

"Not yet."

"Well, call her. I'm getting tired of her ringing my fucking doorbell."

"I got nothing to talk with her about."

"Why, you think ducking her looks good?"

"Fuck them... they're the biggest crooks –"

"Talk to this lady and get it over with. You're making it worse for everyone."

"Who's everyone, you?"

"You're damn right... call her!" Squalo struts away.

CHAPTER 11

The next morning, Nutsy is at the sports park gazing around. It's not that this is a pleasant site to visit, but it seems to take his mind off of things. In a way, it is soothing to him. It's hard to explain and no one would probably understand but standing at this spot takes Nutsy's mind into a different world. A world that is much different than his everyday life.

Miguel wanders by with a few of his associates. He catches eyes with Nutsy and just nods. It was a half ass nod but at least he acknowledged him. Nutsy gives him a nod back and watches these men roam down the side of the field pointing to areas while plotting out their project.

As of now, a final decision has not been made by the board. Nutsy still needs one more member to even the vote out. The lady is still on the fence and is leaning toward the condo project since it seems to be the safer bet for the city.

Billy has been trying his hardest to persuade her decision. Even the mayor has been, but since she has the power to cast her own vote, she is going to make sure it's exactly what she believes in.

She does love Nutsy's proposal but is not sold on the total cost and sustainability of it. The condo project is much simpler to grasp and understand. Plus, the residential market has been on fire lately, so filling the units should not be an issue.

Nutsy is not sure how this will all play out anyway. Although he hasn't been drinking or smoking cigars lately, he still gets occasional twinges in his chest. Not as much but still enough to be noticeable to him. He still refuses to see Munchie though. Maybe he is afraid of what he might hear or maybe, he needs to stay focused on a bigger task.

At this point, Nutsy's issues with Squalo seem minuscule since O'Leary has been leaning on him and Leo is still creating more issues by the week.

Nutsy is also still dealing with his children's situations. His daughter is still considering leaving to join the Navy and his son is unhappy in the facility he is back at.

Nutsy sometimes toys with the idea of packing everything in and heading south. He has always been a man with tremendous willpower, but he's feeling tired and on edge all the time now. He tries to retain his charismatic personality but even that is becoming a struggle lately.

While he gazes toward the field, Nutsy wonders how his life turned out the way it has. Not that he's complaining, but if he wasn't that quick with numbers, maybe he would've headed down a different path in life. He thinks about the time he was around twenty-one. He was passing by a few older bookies playing bocce ball in a local park.

One of the guys had heard about how fast Nutsy could count and yelled out, "Hey you! Come here a minute!"

FOUR SQUARE MILES, *the final project*

Nutsy had on jeans and the Zeppelin tee-shirt he usually wore. He loved Zeppelin back then and would play their vinyl albums on his cheap turntable any chance he got. He would change it up with some Halen, Maiden, and Floyd from time to time. "You talkin' to me?" Nutsy asked while turning toward the guys.

One of the guys whispered, "What does this kid have an attitude now?"

The bookie held up his hand to tell his friend to relax. "Yeah, I heard you're pretty good with numbers."

"So?" At this point in his life, Nutsy was busting his ass working construction for a local contractor and getting paid minimum wage off the books.

The bookie whipped out a large stack of bills and said, "I'll bet you that you can't figure out how much is here within a minute."

"That will take me about thirty seconds. How much ya wanna bet?" This was the biggest stack of cash Nutsy had ever seen in his life. He was working for a measly salary to help support his mother and sister at that time and this stack surely could have gone a long way.

"I'll bet you whatever is here." The bookie waived the stack of cash in Nutsy's face to entice him.

Another bookie said, "Leave 'im alone… he doesn't look like he has two pennies to rub together."

Nutsy knew very well he didn't have anywhere close to the amount in this stack, but he knew he could do it. If there was one thing he was good at, it was counting, and quickly. He already won a few wagers from friends who didn't believe it either.

So, he nodded since he was up to the challenge. He took the thick stack of cash from the bookie and moved to a wooden picnic table close by. He took a seat to get comfortable.

Once he was ready, he nodded to the bookie to start off the time. The bookie gave Nutsy a signal and Nutsy started flicking through the stack while whispering the count to himself. The bookies watched in amazement how fast his hand flew through the stack, but they still did not believe he'd get the amount right.

The longer he counted, the faster Nutsy's hand flicked through the pile. It was no different than how he counts today.

Once he got to the last bill, Nutsy placed it down and said, "Two thousand four hundred and eight five." That seemed like a million dollars to him at that time. He couldn't believe he was staring at that much money.

The other bookies glanced toward their friend waiting for his response. He couldn't believe Nutsy had gotten the correct amount that quickly. He was debating whether he should admit it or not, but a bet was a bet, and he knew your word meant everything back then.

Another bookie shrugged and asked his speechless friend, "So, is he right or what?"

He eventually nodded yes. So Nutsy stood up, gathered the cash together, shoved it in his front pocket and said, "Have a nice day."

One of the bookies said, "Whoa, not so fast, kid."

Nutsy paused for a second. He had a feeling maybe he insulted this group of respected and feared men. He stood speechless waiting for one of them to make their move, but his thoughts were quite the opposite. "You wanna job, kid?"

"You're offering me a job? To do what?"

"Exactly what you just did. And maybe a few other things here and there."

"How much ya offering?"

"I'm offering you a career, kid. A chance to work with the big players of this city."

Nutsy stared at these men who were all dressed impeccably. He thought for a second how nice it would be to go to work like that everyday instead of how he was dressed. He envisioned walking into a tailor's shop with a few brand new suits.

He wasn't completely sold on the offer though. The bookie still didn't give him a figure and he needed money for his mother and sister. He was more concerned about their well-being than even his own during that time. After all, he became the man of the house at a young age.

After Nutsy didn't answer, the bookie said out loud, "So be it, kid. Hopefully, you make it home with all that cash."

He turned around to finish his game of bocce ball with his friends.

"I asked ya how much? Unless the big players are gonna personally pay my family's rent?"

The bookie turned back and puffed on his cigar. He stared at Nutsy and thought for a second then replied, "I'll double whatever you're making busting your hole to make ends meet."

"When do I start?"

"As soon as you buy new clothes. You wanna work with us, you're gonna have to clean up first."

Nutsy nodded and offered his hand for a handshake. "I'm Nuccio Gento."

"I know who you are. I'm Salvatore DeSanto, they call me Squalo around here."

Another bookie said, "He's the kid who used to drop off slips for his mother, remember?"

A few beeps from a car breaks Nutsy's thoughts, and he turns to see Ladro sitting in his car. "You said a half hour, right?" Ladro asks.

Nutsy heads toward the car and gets into the passenger seat. "I still think we coulda squeezed another field in."

"How about we get the approval first?"

"Yeah, I'm starting to think it ain't ever gonna happen."

The car takes off down a one-way street and Ladro replies, "Have faith… on another note, the Agent came in again looking for you. I gotta say, she's pretty hot."

"Yeah, it's the hot ones ya gotta be careful with. Ya get sidetracked and next thing ya know you're behind bars. Stop at Maddie's. Papo called. He wants to meet."

Leo had to make a quick stop at the bank to discuss his loan application. He is currently sitting at Belinda's desk annoyed since the bank wants additional information again. They are now asking for income statements from the business, and personal bank statements. Belinda knows firsthand that Leo cannot produce them, and she told him to pull the application.

She is trying to explain to Leo that the information needed is part of the review process and bank procedures, but he doesn't want to hear it. Leo just wants Belinda to somehow push the loan through.

Blackie notices the tone of their conversation escalating and decides to head over since the customers are curiously glancing over wondering what the ruckus is all about. "What's the problem here?" Blackie asks Leo with a stern tone.

"This bank is the problem. Since when is all this shit needed?"

"Things are different today. It's bank policy."

"Policy my ass. You're both just busting my balls now." Leo replies with an escalating tone.

"Once you get the information, you can bring it back. Until then, there's nothing she can do."

"Says who?"

"Me, that's who."

Leo stands up and leans in toward Blackie's face. "Push it through… and I haven't forgotten about my money either."

Agent O'Leary walks into the bank and notices Leo in Blackie's face. She heads over toward them and says, "Leonardo DeSanto. What a surprise."

Leo replies, "What?" He has no idea it's Agent O'Leary and she catches him off guard while he turns around.

"I'm starting to wonder about you. It seems you've been ducking me."

"I've been busy and have no time for your bullshit." Leo is still annoyed about his loan.

"Well, I have some more questions to ask."

"I can't right now. I have a meeting to attend."

"Then when can you?"

"Tonight, stop by my father's place again. You seem to know the place very well." Leo heads out without waiting for her reply.

Blackie heads toward her office and Agent O'Leary calls out, "Maria?"

Blackie turns and asks, "How do you know my name?"

"You don't remember me, do you?"

"Not really."

"Tara O'Leary."

Blackie's eyes open wide.

Nutsy, Ladro, and Papo are in Maddie's Tavern on the north side. They are sitting in a booth toward the back by themselves discussing the increase of violence in the city.

Papo does not like the publicity their city is currently receiving and is becoming anxious since he has investors to answer to. More concerning, is his brother's boss on the Island.

Papo promised Paulie's boss many years ago that he and a few other key players control this city and if things start turning for the worse, it would be easily corrected. Paulie's boss knows very well that Leo is out of jail and is probably the reason the Feds have been around. Things have been quiet for years and big money has been made, but even larger money is on the line right now.

The waitress pauses by the table and Papo says, "One more round and then we'll leave you alone."

The waitress smiles and asks, "Are you having one this time, Nutsy?"

"Nope."

"Papo replies, "Come on. Just have one with us."

"I told ya guys, I quit drinking."

Papo asks Ladro, "Is this guy for real, or what?"

Ladro replies, "I have to say, I think he is this time."

The waitress smiles and says, "Good for you, Nutsy." She heads toward the next table.

Ladro whispers, "That was a nice little look she gave you."

Papo replies, "I asked her out already."

Nutsy asks, "And what did she say?"

"I'm not her type."

Ladro replies, "It's the beard."

"Nah, the ladies love the beard today," Papo replies.

Nutsy cuts in, "Alright, forget the beard… let's get back to where we left off."

Papo says, "Before this place starts crawling with more Feds, we gotta do it."

"There's already too many eyes on this guy right now."

"I told you, we should've taken care of him as soon as he was released," Papo replies and then finishes off his beer.

Nutsy replies, "I was hoping he learned his lesson in the cage."

Papo asks, "Aren't you the one who always says a leopard never changes its spots?"

Ladro laughs and replies, "I just told him the same thing a few months ago."

The waitress approaches the table and places two beers down. Ladro has to break horns and asks her, "Let me ask you something. Are beards in?"

Papo's eyes roll.

The waitress replies, "It depends on the guy." She smiles and walks away.

Ladro stands up and says, "You're fucked. Shave it off."

Papo asks, "What do you mean?"

"You can't figure it out? I'll be right back" Ladro laughs and heads toward the bathroom.

Papo says, "This guy always talks in riddles."

Nutsy nods to acknowledge his comment and says, "Listen, I didn't wanna say this in front of Ladro, but this new agent can ruin us."

"There's no proof of anything. No cameras, no witnesses. Nothing."

"Still, if she pulls this case back out from under the rug, a lot of heads are gonna turn."

"That's why Leo's gotta go. The faster he does, the faster she leaves."

"It ain't that simple anymore, Papo. This city has cameras all over now."

"Well, it better get figured out soon. Some of your investors are becoming concerned."

"Who?"

"It doesn't matter who. They're starting to feel the risk is greater than the reward… I'm just being upfront with you."

Nutsy glances away and notices Ladro heading back toward the table.

Papo continues, "Do you think anyone from your old club could take care of this?"

"Nah, I haven't been there in over ten years."

"Too bad, that would be perfect."

Ladro takes a seat and asks, "What would be perfect?"

Blackie is now rehashing the past with Agent O'Leary in her office. They are discussing the days they had taken karate class together and the many spars they had. Blackie had usually gotten the best of Agent O'Leary, but she is incredibly quick and skilled too.

Nutsy paid for Blackie's classes back then since it was part of their bargain for Blackie to leave the group she was involved with. She worked her way quickly up to black belt status just like Agent O'Leary had done. So, they have a lot in common.

Agent O'Leary says, "Alright, I'm glad we had the chance to catch up, but I need to discuss something important with you."

"Sure, anything."

"I like your brother, I do. But I have a feeling I'm going to eventually have to take him in. And I really don't wanna have to do that."

"Why? He hasn't done anything wrong."

"We want Leo off the streets. I'm asking your brother to help me out, but he doesn't seem to want to cooperate."

"Listen, it's no secret my brother and Leo never got along, but he's not a rat, Tara."

"Fair enough. How about you? Do you know anything that could help me out?"

"I don't associate myself with Leo anymore. Way before he went to jail."

"How about his sister? Do you think she would know anything?"

"Nah, they have a shitty relationship. Leo wouldn't tell her anything."

"One last thing. The insurance carrier thinks Leo's place might have been torched. Is his sister capable of doing something like that?"

"Nah, no way. She's not that type."

"If you hear anything, let me know." She slides her business card across the desk. "And anytime you'd like to spar, give me a ring. We'll see if you still have it or not."

"Oh, I have it. Trust me."

"That's what they all say."

It was Nutsy's turn to go to the bathroom at Maddie's, so Ladro and Papo are sitting in the booth together finishing their last beer. Papo is becoming concerned about Nutsy and asks, "Is anything going on with Nutsy?"

"Like what?"

"The guy ain't drinking, the guy ain't smoking. I haven't even heard one curse word from him in a while."

Ladro laughs and replies, "I don't know for sure, but I think he's trying to change his ways."

"For what?"

Nutsy approaches the booth so Ladro does not answer Papo's question. "Let's get outta here. I'm tired of watchin' ya guys drink."

Papo nods and replies, "You know the price of turf just went up ten percent, right."

"With our luck, by the time this thing ever gets approved, we'll probably pay double to put this up."

"Welcome to the world of a contractor."

Ladro replies, "Maybe, the turf might have to fall off a truck too?"

Nutsy sarcastically replies, "Yeah, thousands of yards all over the Hutch… come on, let's go."

Agent O'Leary stands up to get ready to leave Blackie's office and says, "Your niece has a lot of potential. Did she ever consider being a fed?"

"I don't think so."

"I gotta say, she's strong and powerful. I could see her involved in professional competitions one day. Her punches are explosive."

"Yeah, I know. Before she hurt her ankle, I was working out with her in my basement. How long have you been running the school?"

"About ten years now. Stop by one day." Agent O'Leary heads out.

Belinda watches Agent O'Leary leave the bank and quickly heads into Blackie's office. "Who was that?"

"A Fed."

"Why is a Fed around here?"

"It seems that your brother is creating a mess again."

"Did she ask anything about his shop?"

Blackie just nods yes and Belinda sighs.

CHAPTER 12

It's 6:30 pm and Squalo is sitting with Leo in his kitchen discussing their situation with Agent O'Leary. Squalo is annoyed that Leo seems to be downplaying their dilemma, but Leo is becoming annoyed that Squalo keeps questioning him about it.

It is troubling to Squalo and he's repeating the same thing over and over. Leo says with an annoyed tone, "I told you, just keep your fucking mouth closed."

"I'm telling you right now, if push comes to shove, I'm not going down because of all your bullshit."

The doorbell buzzes and Squalo stands up, "And if this passes over, you better wake the fuck up."

Squalo heads toward the door and opens it. Agent O'Leary is standing in the hallway and says, "Please tell me he's here, because if he's –"

"I'm right here," Leo replies while standing behind Squalo.

"Good. Where are we doing this?" Agent O'Leary asks.

Leo replies, "It doesn't matter to me. It's up to the old man."

Squalo replies, "Let's sit in the dining room like adults, alright?"

Agent O'Leary nods and Squalo opens the door to let her in. Leo doesn't wait for anyone and heads toward the dining room by himself. Squalo at least allows Agent O'Leary to walk before him like a gentleman.

They both walk into the dining room and Agent O'Leary takes a seat across from Leo while Squalo takes a seat at the head of the table. She peeks over toward the empty shark tank and asks, "What happened to the tank?"

Squalo replies, "It's a long story that you probably wouldn't care to hear."

Agent O'Leary peeks around and notices the floor buckling around the tank. "I guess a leak, ha?"

"Good guess," Squalo replies but remains short with his answer.

Leo becomes impatient since he is looking to meet a few people downtown and asks, "Are you here to discuss the tank, or what?"

Squalo bites his lip. He cannot believe Leo started off their conversation like this.

"Actually no, I'm not. I'm here because of the mess you've been creating."

"You're not dealing with a rookie. Ask me what you want instead of fishing."

"The first night you got out, where were you?"

"Probably getting laid somewhere."

Squalo puckers his lips.

Leo continues, "I stopped by the shop and was with my father the rest of the night."

Agent O'Leary glances toward Squalo and asks, "Is that the case?"

Squalo just nods. This is what he was concerned about, getting pulled into Leo's predicament.

"Did you have any contact with Vito?"

"I don't know any Vito," Leo replies.

"The one that worked in your shop."

"I don't know any of the workers. My sister and father handled them."

Agent O'Leary asks Squalo, "Did you know him?"

"I heard of him around town. That's about it."

"A few witnesses place him in your car with the other guy… Dona… whatever his name is."

"We might've given him a ride one day. That's about it."

"Might've? I think that's something you would remember."

"I do a lot of running around, Agent O'Leary."

"How about Detective Dons? Either of you know him?"

Squalo replies, "Of course. The most crooked detective in Four Square. Why?"

Agent O'Leary blows off the question and asks Leo, "What about you?"

"Sure. Everyone knows that dirty detective. Why are you asking?"

"I'm sure you both know by now."

Both Squalo and Leo shrug and remain quiet.

"His head was splattered all over his front seat."

Leo replies with a sarcastic tone, "Shit, that's too bad. What a fucking shame."

Squalo instantly thinks Leo might have something to do with Dons by his reaction. He knows Leo had illegal dealings with Dons from years back. "It's not surprising. He wasn't a liked guy." Squalo tries to take a much calmer approach.

"So, neither one of you know anything about this?"

They both shake their heads no and shrug it off.

"Lastly, the shop."

Leo asks, "What about it?"

"Maybe you can explain this." O'Leary slides a copy of the envelope across the table toward Leo.

Leo takes a glimpse and slides it back. "Never seen it before."

Agent O'Leary slides the envelope toward Squalo, "How about you?"

Squalo takes a glimpse and slides it back. "Nope."

"This check somehow got lost for a few months and then reappeared."

"It sounds like your question is for the post office, not us," Leo replies.

"That's my next stop." Agent O'Leary slides a photo across the table toward Leo. "You know this guy?"

Leo takes a glimpse and slides it back. "Yeah, an old friend."

"What were you talking to him about?"

"Just saying hello since I was in the neighborhood."

"Is that why you both went outside to chat? To catch up on old times?"

"Why, is it a crime to talk to a friend on a sidewalk?"

"I guess we'll be finding out." Agent O'Leary stands up. "And just so you know, this is fraud on top of murder. Thank you for your time." Agent O'Leary walks away.

Kathy is busy hustling around the house preparing for the family's Christmas party coming up in a few days. Since she took off the week before and after Christmas, she signed N-J out from his facility so he can spend time at home with the family. He is always glad to be home, but this time he seems a little different. He's been quiet and not his usual self.

Sammy and N-J are currently sitting at the kitchen table discussing Sammy's graduation. N-J remembered his last year of school and is excited for Sammy. He is asking about her cap and gown and if the colors are still the standard maroon and gold colors of the school. Sammy told him yes and went on to discuss her potential plans at Seaside after the graduation.

N-J never had the opportunity to go to Seaside. He remembers the argument he had with his mother and father regarding this. Neither one of them were comfortable with him going down there for the weekend of drinking, but N-J's glad Sammy will have the opportunity to.

Kathy opens the refrigerator and says, "Sammy, I need you to pick up a few things for me later at the store."

"Can I go too?" N-J asks.

Kathy replies, "Sure, as long as it's alright with your sister?"

Sammy replies, "Of course it is."

Agent O'Leary stops by the counter at the post office and asks for Benny. Benny immediately becomes nervous and asks, "I'm Benny. Who's asking?"

Agent O'Leary holds up her badge and says, "I'm Agent O'Leary. I'd like to have a few words with you."

"I'll meet you on the side." Benny nervously walks through a large room in the back of the lobby and out a side door to meet her. "What can I help you with?"

Agent O'Leary shows Benny the same photo she had shown Leo and asks, "You know this guy?"

Benny nods but remains quiet.

"What were you two discussing?"

"Did I do anything wrong?"

"Not that I'm aware of. Why, did you?"

"Not at all. He just stopped by to say hello I guess."

"You guess?"

"No, I mean, I don't guess. That's what he did." Benny stumbles over his words.

"Okay." Agent O'Leary hands Benny a business card and says, "If you think of anything else, give me a call."

"Why, what would I be thinking about?"

Agent O'Leary pulls out a copy of the envelope. "Did he give you this?"

Benny takes a glimpse and replies, "I don't recall."

"Thank you for your time." Agent O'Leary walks away.

Benny just stares toward O'Leary with a concerned look and senses she has an idea that his answers do not add up.

Leo has become paranoid and is hiding across the street from the post office with sunglasses and a hat on. He watches Agent O'Leary head down the sidewalk. He glances toward the streetlight to see if he can spot a camera since he's wondering where O'Leary got the picture of him and Benny.

It's about 4:30 in the afternoon and Sammy and N-J are standing online at Rotta's Deli when Agent O'Leary walks in to get a quick sandwich. She has been extremely busy making her rounds and eats out most of the time.

Agent O'Leary notices Sammy and says, "You and Bono haven't been around lately." She assumes Nutsy put an end to her going to the karate school.

"Bono has been down south. His father isn't doing too well."

"Oh wow, sorry to hear that... who's this handsome young man with you?"

"My brother."

"Oh, I didn't realize you had a brother." Agent O'Leary extends her hand out for a handshake. "Hi, I'm Agent O'Leary. A friend of your sister."

N-J shakes her hand but does not respond. He's awkward when it comes to introductions and just stares toward the ground.

"N-J, say hello," Sammy says.

N-J peeks up toward Agent O'Leary and says, "Hello." He looks back down.

"I didn't mean to embarrass you," Agent O'Leary says.

"He's not good with hellos," Sammy replies.

"Well, I look forward to seeing you again at class."

"Me too."

Agent O'Leary moves toward the back of the line. Sammy and N-J grab their bags from the owner and head out of the store.

After getting a sandwich from Rotta's deli, Agent O'Leary heads into Sista again and notices Nutsy and Ladro sitting at the bar. Nutsy notices her approaching and sarcastically says, "I'm tellin' ya, people are gonna start talkin' about us around here."

"I told you already, you're not my type. I'm sorry to interrupt your drink, but can I have a word with you in private?"

Ladro replies, "Yeah, you're interrupting his diet soda."

Nutsy stands up and heads toward the same table they have been discussing business at. "I should reserve this spot just for you and me," Nutsy sarcastically says.

They both take a seat and Agent O'Leary asks, "You're sitting at a bar drinking diet soda?"

"I quit drinking. What mind games are we playin' with each other today?"

"I'm just checking to see if you have anything new for me?"

"I told ya, I'm just a man tryin' to make ends meet."

"Sure, with your black two-seater Benz parked outside. What is that about, a hundred grand?"

"No clue, it's a lease."

"I met your son earlier in a deli with your daughter. He's a handsome boy. He must take after your wife."

Nutsy laughs at the comment and replies, "Yeah, thank God, ha?"

"It looks like he needs you around… it would be a shame if you couldn't be there for him."

Nutsy's smile disappears. Agent O'Leary notices and continues, "I guess I finally got your attention."

"What we discuss here is our business. My kids stay out of it. Do I make myself clear?"

"Threatening a federal agent now, ha?" They both stare at each other for a moment. It appears O'Leary has hit a nerve.

"Threats are for children. Action is for adults. Don't confuse them. Besides, I have no business dealings with that degenerate since you let him out," Nutsy throws out a dig with a serious tone.

"I have to admit. This might sound crazy, but I like you and your family. Please don't force me to have to take you away from them."

Nutsy doesn't reply and Agent O'Leary stands up. "I'll be expecting your cooperation soon. I hope I make MYSELF clear." She walks away but then turns, "By the way, how is your shoulder doing?"

"Fine. Why?"

Agent O'Leary walks back to the table and says, "I know you don't believe in coincidences. So, I'll assume you being the only one that took a bullet that day, was your wakeup call."

"I'm not following you."

"Come on, Nuccio. You're much smarter than that." Agent O'Leary walks away.

"Ya like gettin' into people's heads, ha?"

"Only when I have to." She continues walking away.

She pauses by Ladro at the bar and asks, "Are you Lawrence, one of the ten thieves from Harlem?"

Ladro turns and replies, "Are you the good-looking agent everyone's been talking about?" Ladro gives her a smile.

"You know some of those heists are still unsolved, right?"

Ladro remains quiet and she continues, "Wow, I'm not sure whose smile disappeared quicker, yours or your friend's… enjoy your drink." Agent O'Leary heads toward the door.

CHAPTER 13

It's the night of Nutsy and Kathy's Christmas party. Family and friends are slowly piling into Nutsy and Kathy's house for their annual cocktail gathering. It is Saturday night, and a fresh blanket of snow is illuminating the outside lights that are covering their shrubs.

Nutsy would like to enjoy the night but has been getting pulled away by everyone with their own concerns. Billy and Gloria are standing in the kitchen with big smiles. Their relationship seems to be heading in a more serious direction.

Belinda and Munchie are sitting on the living room couch together enjoying a cocktail. They seem to be doing just fine since Belinda started her new job.

A few of the big city players are around such as Papo and Paulie. Tiffany has finally showed her face around town. She spends most of her time at her duplex apartment in lower Manhattan since its close to her office on Wall Street. The full Quad is intact tonight, the real money players of Four Square.

So far Nutsy has been quiet through the night. He's been thinking about Agent O'Leary and the comments she's been making during their conversations. He cannot quite figure her out yet and it's troubling him since Nutsy is usually a good reader of people.

Tiffany, the Manhattan hedge fund manager, walks up to Nutsy in the living room and asks, "Nutsy, can I have a word with you in private?"

"Of course."

They step outside the house and stand right by the front door. "I'm glad ya came, Tiffany. I haven't seen ya around for a while."

"It's nice to see everyone again. Including you, Nutsy. My father would be so happy right now seeing what you're trying to do with the park."

"Hey, I still haven't gotten the votes yet. So, what's up?"

"What's this rumor I hear that you have heart issues?"

"I'm fine. There are no issues. Why?"

"I heard it has a few board members concerned."

"About what?"

"That you're not going to be able to handle the stress. These projects suck out a lot of energy and time."

"Nah, I'll be fine. Do I look alright?"

"To me you do. But you always did."

"You tell them this guy ain't ready to go down."

Tiffany smiles and replies, "I will… I reviewed the statements. Where are you getting the profits from?"

"Estimates based on similar complexes this one will be like."

"How?"

"You can see online how many teams sign up for their tournaments every week. We're planning on doing at least that here."

Tiffany nods and the door swings open. "Oh, there you are," Kathy says while standing by the doorway.

"Yeah, what's up?"

"My father's looking for you."

"Go ahead. We'll finish this later." Tiffany heads back inside.

Nutsy follows her in and then approaches Billy and Gloria in the kitchen. "Ya needed me?"

Billy says to Gloria, "I'll be right back." He gives her a peck on the lips and walks away with Nutsy. They stand by the side of the dining room and Nutsy asks, "What's going on?"

"She was tough, but I think I finally got her."

"Who?"

"The last board member."

"Are ya sure?"

"I'm pretty sure. Between you and me, I think she has something to do with that agent that keeps poking around."

"Like what?"

"I think they're together."

"What do ya mean, like a couple?"

"I think… I'm not a hundred percent though."

"Wow, I didn't see this one coming."

"I know, me either. She still bothering you?"

Nutsy nods yes.

"Just keep quiet and don't say anything… on a different note, I want you to be my best man."

"For what?"

"I'm proposing to Gloria soon."

"What?!"

"Hey, I guess when you know, you know. Just keep it quiet for now."

Papo and Paulie approach them and Papo says, "This looks like a meeting of the minds."

"Yeah, two shot minds," Nutsy sarcastically replies.

"Speak for yourself. We'll finish this later, Nutsy." Billy replies and walks away.

Paulie says, "Nice party like always, Nutsy."

"I'm glad ya enjoyin' yourself."

"Papo told me we have a creeper roaming around town now."

Nutsy replies, "It seems that way."

"We screwed up not taking The Lion right out."

Nutsy replies, "Let it play out."

Paulie asks, "And just give this guy free reign to do whatever he pleases? It could be anyone next, even you."

"What do ya want me to say, Paulie?"

"What is it with you, ha?"

Nutsy smiles and says, "Come on. Enough of this guy. I'm tryin' to enjoy the night." Nutsy walks away.

Paulie says to Papo, "Is it me or is this guy picking the wrong time to change his ways?"

The rest of the night was spent drinking and eating. Nutsy of course still had the thoughts of the park and Agent O'Leary on his mind. He did his best to mingle although he did not have one drink all night. Even Kathy was surprised he didn't drink for their annual Christmas Party.

It's now about one in the morning and everyone has been slowly filtering out. Billy and Gloria are the last to leave. Gloria is feeling good and approaches Nutsy by the front door. "I really had a great time." She gives him a kiss on the cheek.

"I'm glad to hear it." Nutsy shakes Billy's hand and asks, "You okay to drive?"

"I'm good. We'll talk tomorrow."

After leaving the party, Billy and Gloria get into Billy's car and then drive away.

Kathy says to Nutsy, "Well, another Christmas party down."

"I haven't seen N-J all night. Where is he?"

"Upstairs. You know he doesn't care for crowds."

Nutsy wanders into N-J's room and notices him glancing at a book while sitting on his bed. "What are ya reading?" Nutsy asks.

"Your book about Nettles… was he really that great of a fielder?"

"The best I've ever seen at the corner. He had reflexes like a cat."

"I miss playing, dad."

Nutsy takes a seat at the edge of the bed and says, "I wanted to talk to ya when the time was right. No one in this house is avoiding you. Ya know that, right?"

"You and mom said I would be able to stay home and now I can't."

"Did she tell ya why?"

"She said you have something to do, and she can't leave her job yet."

"I might have an issue with my heart, that's why."

"What kind of issue?"

"I don't know yet. I didn't have the test done."

"You and mom have to be around for me as long as you can."

"Ya don't have to worry about that. We both will."

"Why haven't you had the test done yet?"

Nutsy is at a lost for words and N-J senses there is more to this than what Nutsy says. "You can die from this like grandpa did, can't you?"

Nutsy doesn't respond since he truly doesn't know the answer himself.

"You always told me to follow my heart, and it's your own that you're not taking care of."

"It's not that simple, N-J."

"A man without a heart, could never be a true man… do you remember telling me that?"

Nutsy rubs N-J's head and replies, "Ya remember that one, ha?"

"To this day, papa… your heart needs help. If you don't fix it, you could never be true again."

Nutsy just smiles. He knows his son's thoughts are innocent and true. If only life could be this simple. In a certain way for N-J it is, and Nutsy thinks about how truly special this must be for him.

Billy is driving home with Gloria and they stop at a red light a few minutes away from Nutsy's house. "Your place or mine?" Billy asks.

"How about yours this –"

BANG. BANG. BANG. The passenger window explodes, glass shatters all over the front seat.

Billy frantically spins the steering wheel and his car smashes into a parked car. Car tires screech nearby, and a car peels away. The parked car's alarm engages and echoes down the quiet street.

After an ambulance arrived at the scene and took Billy and Gloria to the hospital, Kathy received a call at home. Nutsy and Kathy both raced to the hospital. Billy was not hit too badly, but Gloria took a few shoots to the side of her shoulder.

A few hours later, Benny stumbles out of a bar on the east side of the city. It's a small local bar and caters to residents of the immediate area. He is feeling good and whistling a song to himself while heading toward his parked car down the street.

He finally makes it to his car and places the key into the door to open it. He pauses since he knows it's probably not a good idea to drive in his condition.

Since his residence is only four blocks away, Benny decides to be responsible and walk home. He heads down the quiet, dark street whistling to himself again.

It's now about 7am and Nutsy slurps down his coffee while sitting at the island in his kitchen. He just arrived back home after being at the emergency room all morning long.

Kathy went back to her father's place to keep him company since he was distraught over the incident and couldn't sleep anyway.

A week has gone by and Billy and Gloria seem to be doing fine. Gloria is still rattled from the incident, but Billy is steaming from it. His thoughts have been changing regarding Leo and how he needs to be handled. The authorities do not seem be able to nab Leo and Billy is not confident they will until someone close to him dies.

Blackie and Sammy are now on their way to Agent O'Leary's karate school. She invited them both up to work out and figured it would be a great time to spar with Blackie. There are no classes until later this afternoon, so they have plenty of time to work on their skills.

They are now all in the gym area. Agent O'Leary is dressed in her uniform with a black belt wrapped tightly around her waist. Sammy has on sweats and a t-shirt. Blackie pulls out her gear from a gym bag, slips down her black jeans, and puts on her uniform. She wraps her black belt around her waist and tightens the knot.

They all stand in the middle of the room and bow toward each other before beginning their workout. Sammy is trying to follow Blackie and Agent O'Leary while they perform their individual katas. Their motions are precise with intense stares on their faces.

After performing their katas, they all begin working out with one another. Blackie and Agent O'Leary both show

Sammy some of their kick moves. They are similar in flexibility and height, but Blackie seems to be a tad bit quicker than O'Leary is. Only an experienced person would be able to notice it though.

Agent O'Leary is extremely impressed with Sammy like always. She can notice the raw power and natural strength she has. She just needs to gain some more flexibility in her toned legs to be able to kick like Blackie and O'Leary can.

Agent O'Leary asks Sammy, "Have you ever considered working for the bureau?"

"What bureau?"

"The federal bureau?"

"Not really. I don't think I would have a chance to." Sammy knows very well what her father does and never considered it to be an option.

"If you ever decide to consider it, I'll put in a good word for you."

"I'll keep that in mind… I'm still thinking of applying to be a Seal."

"I just figured I'd throw it out there… would you mind if I go a few rounds with your aunt?"

"Not at all." Sammy was hoping to see them both spar in real action.

"What do you say, Maria?"

"Hey, why not. I'm here, right?"

FOUR SQUARE MILES, *the final project*

O'Leary walks to the side of the room and picks up shin pads and small fighting gloves. She hands Blackie a pair and says, "Here, put these on."

"Wow, this is different. We never wore these before."

"Yeah well, I have no choice. It's different today."

Blackie and O'Leary stand in the middle of the room and bow toward each other. They then get into their fighting stances and dance around a bit. "It's been a while for me," Blackie says.

O'Leary spins with her leg in the air, connects across Blackie's cheek. Blackie takes a few steps backwards and says, "I guess we're going full blown, ha?"

"Hey, I don't get to spar with black belts too often." O'Leary smiles.

"Okay, if you say so." Blackie sets in her stance. She peeks toward Sammy, gives a quick wink. She takes a few steps to the left, but then quickly steps right, spins with lightning speed with her leg in the air. SMACK, across the side of O'Leary's head.

O'Leary stumbles backwards and says, "I see you still got speed."

"If I was blessed with anything, it was speed… maybe some looks too." Blackie smiles.

Sammy watches them in amazement. She cannot believe the shots they both are taking from each other and hoping to be as good as either of them one day.

After about fifteen minutes of intense sparring, Blackie and O'Leary decide to call it quits. O'Leary's lip is bleeding and Blackie's eye is puffy after catching an elbow. While heading toward the door to leave, Agent O'Leary says to Blackie, "Don't forget. If you hear anything around town, let me know."

"I will."

"How about we do this again one weekend?" O'Leary asks.

Sammy immediately replies, "I would love to."

"Yeah sure, thanks for the workout," Blackie replies.

Agent O'Leary nods while her cell phone buzzes. "Excuse me one second." She answers her phone, "Agent O'Leary!" She listens and nods, then hangs up. "It looks like another body was found in your town."

CHAPTER 14

Agent O'Leary arrives at the scene close by the west side of town where Benny's body was recently discovered by a resident. His body was stuffed under a large bush in a brushy area, so it was difficult to notice him until someone was close by. He has strap marks around his neck like Big Charlie had.

"So, this is getting interesting. We had a shooting earlier this week and now a guy strangled in this city." Agent O'Leary says to a local police officer.

Agent O'Leary has been getting tremendous pressure from her boss to solve some of these cases, and she knows another strangled body will only cause more friction between them. She figures Miguel would be the easiest to break since he has dealings with Leo already.

After leaving the crime scene, Agent O'Leary heads toward Miguel's office. Miguel is reviewing plans for a new project his firm is working on. He notices O'Leary walking in and asks, "What now?"

She takes a seat in front of his desk and says, "This is it. Your last chance to come clean. My patience is gone."

"If you had something concrete, you wouldn't be asking, you'd be telling me."

"Did you know a postal worker named Bernardo?"

"Yeah, why?"

"He was found strangled earlier this morning. Similar, to how your friend Charles was… who knows, maybe you're next."

"I have nothing to do with either of them."

"I guess we'll find out. Hopefully not the hard way since your friend seems to be covering his tracks very well."

Miguel glances away. He knows damn well this is Leo's doing since he had Benny repay him his favor.

"And why would you even consider Leo as one of your backers? You seem smarter than that."

"How do you know that?"

"Come on, give me more credit than that."

Miguel knows this is not a good situation for himself or his business. Agent O'Leary can notice the nervousness in his eyes. "Leo's going down either way. The question is, will he get to you before we get to him."

Miguel's eyes roam while he's in thought.

Agent O'Leary walks out of Miguel's office after finishing their discussion. Leo happens to be heading toward

Miguel's office when he notices her leaving the building. He turns and heads in the opposite direction to make sure she does not notice him.

Agent O'Leary is now out of Leo's sight, so he wanders into Miguel's office and takes a seat in front of his desk. Miguel doesn't seem as warm and friendly as usual and Leo senses something is not right. "What's she doing here?"

"Who?" Miguel doesn't know Leo saw O'Leary outside.

"That bitch Agent. That's who."

"She was asking about some guy who was found strangled… you know anything about that?"

"Nothing at all. Why is she asking you?"

"I don't know. I was gonna ask you that." Miguel is playing coy. He is not comfortable one bit with how things are progressing.

Leo just stares with his piercing eyes.

"She said the guy was strangled with similar straps you used for Big Charlie."

Leo gets an uncomfortable feeling about this conversation and replies, "I have no idea what you're talking about." He plays it off in case Miguel is cooperating with Agent O'Leary.

Miguel knows Leo is attempting to cover his ass. This is surely a sign of distrust. Miguel becomes uncomfortable himself and replies, "I have bad news. We're probably pulling out of the condo project." Miguel thinks this is the best avenue to take since he feels he will not be able to tell Leo that he cannot be an investor anymore.

"Why? I'm close to getting the money together."

"The other investors aren't comfortable with what's been happening up there. They want me to pull the plug on it."

"Fuck that… that means that prick walks away with the property?"

"Not necessarily. It still needs to get approved by the board and I heard it's not done yet."

"Who are these other investors you're talking about?"

"It's confidential, Leo. Just like you are." There is no way Miguel is giving Leo this information. The last thing Miguel would want is Leo jeopardizing his money source.

Leo stands up and blurts out, "You ain't fucking pulling out of nothing. You tell those pricks I said so."

"Without funding, there's no project. It's that simple, Leo."

Leo stares again. He is not buying the story and Miguel knows it by the look in Leo's eyes. This project was a hot ticket and practically a sure thing. "We'll be talking soon." Leo struts out.

The next morning, Leo hides out in front of Miguel's office waiting to see if Agent O'Leary shows her face again. He has been waiting for a few hours and is ready to leave when he notices her heading toward Miguel's building. He puckers his lips and struts away. He feels there is more to their meetings than what Miguel implies.

Nutsy is in a meeting with Billy and The Quad discussing the project's financing. Gloria has been recuperating nicely from the shooting incident. She has a large bandage down her shoulder but seems to be getting a little stronger every day.

The Quad members are becoming concerned about the escalating violence in the city. Nutsy is still not buying into the fact that he needs to be involved in Leo's disappearance.

In so many words, Papo tells Nutsy he's reneging on his agreement from years ago. Nutsy tells him he doesn't care. He is a changed man and looking to move on with his life in a different direction.

He tells Papo he made the deal when he was a young man and had nothing at that time. Today, he is a family man with everything to lose.

Papo is not thrilled with Nutsy at this moment and is thinking about pulling out of the sports project altogether, even as the general contractor. "This is our city, and no one fucks with it. You remember that one, Nutsy?" This was what Nutsy said to Papo right before they took out the group years back and Papo wants to be certain Nutsy remembers saying it.

"You and me, we'll discuss this in private later."

After the shooting, Billy's thoughts have also changed. "Papo's right, Nutsy. Leo's only gonna make things worse around here and we all know it."

"Both of ya, you're talkin' like ya already know it's him."

Billy asks, "Then you tell us who it is then?"

Paulie chimes in, "I agree one hundred percent. It's The Lion and we gotta have him poached. I'm pulling my guys in."

Papo replies, "No way. This gets handled from the inside. This is what we always agreed on, and that's how it's remaining."

Paulie replies, "Yeah well, I don't see shit happening except bodies getting clipped, and none of them are Leo. So as far as I'm concerned, nothing's getting handled."

Tiffany has been patiently waiting for the bickering to end, but she decides to chime in, "I'm not thrilled with what's happening either. What happens if we all dump big money into this project, and families are afraid to come to this town?"

Nutsy replies, "They'll come. The complex will be directly off the parkway. There would be no reason they'd have to travel through town."

Papo replies, "It's the city's reputation that's on the line. Outside families won't come here just because of it."

Paulie chimes in, "Yeah, Nutsy. Now we got feds roaming around this city. That never happened in the past."

"Sure, it did."

"Not like this. This lady means business," Papo replies.

Nutsy replies, "She's harmless. Trust me."

Tiffany says, "Nutsy, I have to admit, this would be a tough sell to my investors right now. If things don't quiet down around town, I'm afraid I'll have to pass on this one."

"I thought we all agreed on this already?" Nutsy asks.

Tiffany replies, "Nutsy, you know my family has always loved you. But this city has been changing lately and getting bad press. This money I invest comes from my shareholders and right now I can't justify it."

Paulie says to Nutsy, "My boss ain't thrilled with it either. He's on the fence too."

Papo says, "Yeah, and all of this bullshit might even make my towers worthless."

"Come on, what are ya talkin' about? Worthless? I think you're exaggerating now," Nutsy replies.

"Well, until things quiet down around here, it looks like we're on hold for the time being," Papo replies.

Billy nods toward Gloria and asks, "You've been quiet. What's your take?"

"I am a bit concerned. Especially after being shot at. I'm on the fence right now to be honest."

Nutsy stands up and replies, "No problem. You guys don't wanna back me, I'll find other investors." Nutsy heads toward the door.

Papo replies, "Nutsy, we didn't say that."

"No, you're just reneging too." Nutsy walks out and closes the door.

After Nutsy left, everyone else stayed for a while to discuss the project and their concerns. As of now, they all decided to hold back on the funding to see how things develop around the city first.

They do believe in Nutsy's project, but this will take a large amount of funding that no one is willing to risk at this time. They feel that as long as Leo is around, he is going to give this city a bad reputation like he did in the past, which in turn, will jeopardize the families willing to visit this ball field.

After Billy and The Quad left Papo's apartment, Papo calls Ladro who is currently sitting at the conference table in The Headquarters booking football wagers for this upcoming weekend. Ladro hangs up the office phone and answers his cell, "Yeah, Papo?"

"Let me ask you something. Did that infection get to Nutsy's brain?"

"Why do you ask that?"

"What's all this bullshit about that he's trying to change his ways?"

"Oh that… what can I say? The man wants to take a different path in life."

"Different path? We got a major issue with this derelict in this city, and now he decides this?"

"What do you want me to tell you?"

"I want you to talk to him. Put some sense back into his head. This isn't the time for him to soften up. This guy's gotta go."

"He's a grown man, Papo. Life takes us on a different journey sometimes."

"That's bullshit and you know that. Nutsy's a street guy and will always be. I mean, Jesus Christ, the guy ain't even drinking anymore either?"

"Not for months now."

"Well, if he wants his project completed, you better tell him to take his diapers off." Papo hangs up.

Ever since Billy and Gloria were shot at, Billy's thoughts have changed, and he decides to visit Nutsy at The Headquarters. They both take a seat at the bar area to discuss business quietly. Nutsy already knows The Quad is on hold with their funding and is somewhat annoyed, but he has no idea what Billy is currently thinking until now. "I don't see any other way, Nutsy."

"Any other way for what?" Nutsy asks.

"Somehow this guy has to go."

"Yeah sure, ya think he took a shot at you and Gloria and now ya want him gone."

"Who else could it be?"

"It could be anyone, Billy."

"That's bullshit and you know it."

Nutsy just shrugs.

"What are you gonna do? Wait until he takes a shot at you, Kathy, one of your kids?"

Nutsy just stares without a reply.

"Even if you get this project, this guy won't stop. In fact, it will probably set him off more."

"Look, ya know I'm tryin' to be good. Besides, I got this lady up my ass now."

"Can you still shoot long distance?"

Nutsy laughs and replies, "No way. That ain't somethin' ya try on a street after ten years."

CHAPTER 15

Leo now believes his associates are starting to work against him, and he is right. He noticed Agent O'Leary going in and out of Miguel's office a few more times. He can also tell his father's behavior has been changing toward him, since Squalo has not been bickering back and forth with Leo as much.

Agent O'Leary has been putting tremendous pressure on Squalo lately. Upon completing an inspection of his car, the Feds were able to find DNA that led them back to Vito. Agent O'Leary interrogated Squalo about it, but Squalo played it off and said that Vito used to ride in his car from time to time, which is the truth.

Agent O'Leary's main angle is hair fragments belonging to Vito that were found in the trunk of Squalo's car. So, she gave him an ultimatum. She told Squalo to help her and in return, she'll help him. If not, he will rot for a long time for something he probably didn't even do.

Agent O'Leary believes Leo is the cause of the mess being created lately and Squalo is just being a father and trying to cover up for his only son. She does not blame Squalo in a way, but the law is the law, and Squalo can be charged as an accomplice.

Leo is now sitting outside of Sista Bar and Grill in a car and notices Agent O'Leary walk in. He was able to pick-up a cheap car from Miguel's junk yard. He throws on different stolen plates from time to time since the car is not insured or registered. Leo believes Agent O'Leary is relentless and she will not stop. He drives off thinking that she needs to go.

Agent O'Leary walks up to the bar and approaches Nutsy standing with Mucci, the local beer distributor, discussing different craft beers. Nutsy sees O'Leary and says, "Perfect timing. Ya can try out one of my new beers."

"I appreciate the offer, but I don't drink beer. I hate to interrupt, but we need to talk."

Mucci says, "I'll have my guys bring the new IPAs and winter ale." He shakes Nutsy's hand and heads out. He had heard O'Leary was roaming around the city and wanted no part in their conversation.

Nutsy and Agent O'Leary take a seat at the usual table they have been sitting at and Nutsy asks, "How about an apple turnover? They're made fresh everyday."

"I'll try one."

Nutsy holds up two fingers toward the waitress and she nods. Agent O'Leary notices and asks, "She knows?"

"I'm a creature of habit. Everyone knows me like a book around here. I'm sure you're starting to also."

FOUR SQUARE MILES, *the final project* 167

The waitress places an apple turnover in front of O'Leary and Nutsy. "Ya want coffee too?" Nutsy asks.

"Sure." Agent O'Leary glances at the waitress and says, "Thank you."

The waitress smiles and walks away. Agent O'Leary takes a forkful of the apple turnover and nods in enjoyment.

Nutsy says, "See? I told ya you'd like it."

The waitress places two coffee mugs on the table and moves toward the next table.

"So, besides wantin' to see me again, what can I do for ya today?" Nutsy gives a wink.

"Apparently, our friend has been buying a lot of rounds. We believe he's stocking up for something big."

"How do ya know this?"

"Let's just say, someone he has dealings with, flipped."

"Miguel?"

"I can't say… I just thought you should know."

"Why are ya tellin' me this?"

"You got a nice family, Nuccio. I would hate to see something happen to any of them." Besides Nutsy starting to grow on her, she is slowly building a relationship with Blackie and Sammy.

"I appreciate your support for my family, but I have a gut feeling there's more to this visit."

"We both know the way these laws are today. I'll book him and he'll be right back out creating the same havoc."

"So why is that my problem?"

"I'm sure you can see a green light when it's flashing in front of your eyes… thank you for the apple turnover. It was delicious." Agent O'Leary stands up and strolls away.

A week has gone by and Leo is at some abandoned site in the city making another deal with a few sketchy looking individuals. One of the men asks him, "This shit will blow up a block. What the fuck you need this for?"

"It's none of your concern, is it?" Leo snaps back.

"It is if you're fucking with innocent people. We don't need any headaches."

Leo peeks toward the other man who has his hand resting by his belt. He assumes he's packing or at least pretending to be. He thinks about making a move but holds off. Leo assumes the man he is conversing with is also packing and making a move would be too risky. "Nah, I gotta project going on and might need to take down old bleachers."

"Old bleachers? You're buying this shit for bleachers?" The two men burst out in laughter.

Leo hands the guy a pillowcase full of pistols and the guy hands Leo a suitcase full of dynamite. "Have fun with your bleachers." The two men turn away both laughing.

One of the men turns back, chucks a key toward Leo and sarcastically says, "You'll need this to open the suitcase. And don't blow yourself up." Leo thinks about making a move but just squats down and picks up the key.

Leo places the suitcase into the trunk of his car and slams the door closed. "After I take down the whole block, I'll be back for you two dirtbags," Leo mutters to himself. He gets into his car and drives away.

About an hour later, Leo wanders into Squalo's apartment carrying the suitcase and Squalo notices it while watching TV in his living room. "Are you going away or something?" Squalo asks.

"Not anytime soon."

"What's the suitcase for then?"

"I had to buy a few things," Leo replies and heads into the bedroom. He opens the closet door and places the suitcase on the floor. The bottom of the closet is now packed with cardboard boxes of ammo and a few other suitcases. It appears Leo has been busy gathering explosives.

Leo closes the closet door and turns to see Squalo standing behind him. "Whatever is in those boxes, get it the hell out of my apartment." Squalo does not trust Leo at all anymore.

"Don't worry. It will be out soon enough." Leo mutters to himself, "Yeah, everyone thinks I'm a fool. Just because I don't say anything, doesn't mean I don't notice what's going on."

"What the hell are you mumbling about?"

"Yeah, that fuck head wants to kill the project now because he's probably talking. This fucking bitch is roaming all over the place. Knowing you, you're probably talking too." Leo is fired up and his eyes are twitching.

"That's a ridiculous thing to say. Besides, you're the one who brought this all on yourself."

Leo heads into the living room. "You all think I'm a fucking idiot… I'm telling you right now, before I go down, I'm taking everything with me." Leo has lost his cool.

"Are you losing your mind?"

"And you! What the fuck have you ever done for me, ha? Nothing, that's what. All you ever gave a shit about was yourself. Even your own daughter can't stand you."

"You're no good and never were. Even now, you have a second chance and you're still fucking it up."

"Fuck you, old man! You let me rot in that jail cell while you lived in this deluxe apartment. Telling me all these years, you didn't have any money for an attorney. That was all bullshit."

"I don't know what you're up to, but I'm calling the police to get you the fuck out of my apartment once and for all. I ain't going down with you."

"Yeah, why should you? You're just a selfish prick."

"What did you just call me?" Squalo gets in Leo's face.

"You heard me loud and clear. You're a selfish greedy prick… you know something, fuck this." Leo storms into the bedroom again and grabs the suitcase from the closet. He grabs a few other items and shoves them into his pants pocket and other items into his jacket pocket.

Squalo follows behind him and asks, "What the fuck is in that thing?"

Leo's eyes twitch consistently and replies, "If that bookmaker thinks he's gonna parade around the city like a fucking prince, he's mistaken."

Squalo knows very well that when his son's eyes twitch, anything could happen next. He reaches for the suitcase, but Leo yanks it away from him. "Get out of my way."

"I'm not moving."

Leo whips out a 9mm, cocks it, holds it against Squalo's temple and says, "I'm leaving either way. It's your choice."

"Pull it! Go ahead, kill your father while you're at it."

"You were never a father." Leo holds off pulling the trigger, but instead, smashes Squalo across the face with the handle of the pistol. Squalo crashes onto the floor. "This building will be next after Sista if you keep this shit up." Leo throws out a threat.

While Leo moves away, Squalo anxiously yanks out his phone from his pocket and presses Nutsy's number.

Nutsy peeks at his phone while sitting at the conference table in The Headquarters with Ladro and mumbles, "What the hell does he want?" Nutsy answers, "What?"

Squalo replies, "He lost his fucking mind! He's coming for –" Leo smashes a chair over Squalo's head, and the phone falls out of Squalo's hand onto the floor. Leo stomps the phone with his heel and then kicks his father in the stomach while he lies on the ground.

Nutsy asks, "What? What are ya saying?" There is now silence on the other end of the phone since pieces of it are all over the floor.

Leo picks up the suitcase and bolts out of the bedroom leaving Squalo either unconscious or dead on the floor. Either way, he doesn't care. Leo is ready for his mission of destruction since he now feels he has no other avenues.

Nutsy finally hangs up the phone and says to Ladro, "That was strange."

"What happened?"

"I don't know. He just said he lost his mind and he's coming."

"Who's coming?"

Nutsy shrugs and redials Squalo's number. The call goes straight to voicemail again, so Nutsy hangs up. "I don't know." Nutsy thinks about what Agent O'Leary said to him and asks, "Could he be talkin' about Leo?"

"It wouldn't surprise me."

They both stare at each other pondering this over. Nutsy dials Squalo's number again and it goes straight to voicemail. "I don't know, Ladro. I'm gettin' a bad feeling. He was even yellin' on the phone... maybe we should close and get everyone out just in case."

"You really think it's that serious?"

"I don't know, but I'd hate to find out later that it was."

"Alright, let's do it then." Ladro stands up and yells out to the workers, "We gotta shut down early. Grab all your shit and go home."

One of the workers asks, "What happened?"

"We're not sure yet. Just go home for now."

After everyone in The Headquarters left the office upstairs, Nutsy and Ladro head downstairs to clear out the workers and patrons from Sista. One of the bartenders asks Ladro, "What's going on?"

"Not sure yet. We might have a gas leak. Just get out." Ladro does not want to alarm anyone for no reason at all, but he and Nutsy just want everyone safe in case there is an issue.

After everyone cleared out of Sista, Nutsy says to Lado, "I'm going to the house. Go take care of Blackie."

Ladro nods and they both head toward their cars. Nutsy pulls away in his car and calls Kathy who is now home with the kids. Kathy answers, "Yeah, Hun."

"Alright listen, nothing has happened, but I need ya to take the kids and drive away for a while."

"What do you mean drive away?"

"Just get out of the city. Take a ride on the parkway or something."

"Nutsy, what's going on?"

"I don't know. I got a strange call from Squalo before."

"What is he calling you for?"

"I don't know. We got cut off… just get the kids and go."

"What about you?"

"We'll meet up later. Just go. Call your father too." Nutsy hangs up and continues driving down the avenue.

Kathy rounds up Sammy and N-J, and after getting into their car, they jump on the parkway heading north. They both question Kathy about what is happening, and she told them she really does not know herself, that this is what their father wants them to do.

Kathy calls Billy and gets his voicemail. She explains to Billy what Nutsy said. She calls Nutsy and gets his voicemail too. "Everyone has phones, but no one picks up." She hangs up the call and continues driving away.

About a half hour later, Leo pulls up in front of Sista and gets out of his car. The lights inside Sista are still on so it appears open. He pulls the suitcase out of the trunk and heads toward the entrance of Sista.

Leo has an intense glare in his eyes, like he has totally lost it. He is not concerned about knocking off his so-called enemies anymore. He wants mass destruction

FOUR SQUARE MILES, *the final project*

and everyone's livelihoods to be destroyed, starting right here with Nutsy and Ladro's operation.

He pulls on the front door, but its locked so he yanks harder without success. He peeks inside the window to see an empty room and steps back in thought.

A few pedestrians pause to witness his peculiar behavior. They cannot figure out why Leo's swinging his arms back with the suitcase. They have no clue he is winding up to hurl the suitcase through the large pane window, and with his strength, he would have no issue doing it.

One of the pedestrians suddenly realizes what Leo is attempting to do and says, "Hey –"

SPLAT, Leo's head explodes all over the sidewalk and blood sprays the pane window. Pedestrians nervously take cover and glance around. Some anxiously bolt away. Leo's body is lying on the ground and the suitcase is close by. His head has been blown into pieces.

The pedestrian frantically yells out, "Holy shit! Call the cops!" He ducks behind a car just in case another shot is fired. He glances toward Leo and cannot believe The Lion has been taken down this way.

About five minutes later, the street is blocked off by police cars and the sidewalk is roped off. Ladro approaches a police office and asks, "Is that The Lion?"

"It was The Lion."

"Holy shit! What the fuck happened?"

"We have no clue yet."

Nutsy finally makes it to the scene and approaches Ladro. "What the hell happened?"

"Imagine this? Someone took down The Lion."

"Jesus Christ. Did they catch anyone?"

"Not that I know of."

Agent O'Leary approaches Nutsy and Ladro and says, "Don't go too far. We'll need to ask you a few questions." She heads over toward Leo's body.

Residents are in total shock. No one ever believed Leo would be taken down this way. Most are glad to see him gone though.

Ladro asks Nutsy, "We just tell them what we know, right?"

"That's it. We don't know anything else."

Nutsy calls Kathy's number. She is approximately an hour north right now and nervously answers, "I've been calling you. Is everything all right?"

"Yeah, ya can come back now."

"Are you sure?"

"The Lion got taken down on the avenue."

"What, shot?"

"Yeah, in front of the store. It's crazy here right now."

"Did they catch the person?"

"I'm not sure. The Agent is here. She wants to ask me and Ladro questions, so it might be a long night."

"Okay, please be careful."

"Ya speak to your father?"

"I couldn't reach him. I just left a message."

"Alright, keep tryin' 'im."

About two hours later, Nutsy and Ladro are still in the police station with Agent O'Leary. She needs to do her routine work and considering the incident happened right outside of Nutsy's bar and grill, he and Ladro were asked for their cooperation. They both went without hesitation or resistance.

Nutsy is in one room and Ladro in another alone. Agent O'Leary just finished questioning Ladro and is satisfied with his answers. She heads into the next room where Nutsy has been patiently waiting. "Well, your partner seems fine. It's your turn now."

"We have the same answers."

Agent O'Leary takes a seat across from Nutsy and says, "I just have a few concerns. Why didn't you call the police after Salvatore called you?"

"I didn't know what to call about. Our conversation was very vague."

"I guess vague enough for you to clear out the restaurant, ha?"

"That's correct. I didn't wanna be the guy who had an uncomfortable feeling and later found out the hard way."

"You should've called the police, you know."

"Who cares at this point? He got what he deserved. You should be happy too."

"Where did you go when you left?"

"Home."

"Can your family confirm that?"

"They weren't home at the time. After I got the phone call, I told my wife to take the kids and get out."

"So, you told them to leave and went home? That doesn't make any sense to me."

"I'll protect my home to no end. I don't need to jeopardize my family while doing it."

They stare for a moment. "Fair enough. I guess that will be it for now."

"I'll tell ya what, I think we owe whoever did this a trophy. What do ya say?"

She looks into Nutsy's eyes but cannot figure out if he's sincere or not. At this point, his story somewhat makes sense, so she decides to just go along with it.

CHAPTER 16

Later that evening, Nutsy arrives at his house and as soon as he walks into the foyer, Kathy is nervously waiting to see him. The news of what had happened to Leo is buzzing all over the local TV stations.

Kathy wraps her arms around Nutsy tightly. She is just happy to see him. The same with Nutsy. His family means the world to him and he is glad to see everyone home safe and secure.

They both walk into the kitchen where Kathy already had a pot of coffee brewing. Nutsy takes a seat at the island and lets out a big sigh. He pours himself and Kathy a cup of coffee and they both sit in silence for a while. Neither one of them know where this day will take them, but they are both glad to know that Leo is gone.

"Is your father and Gloria good?"

Kathy nods and replies, "Yeah, they're both safe."

About a month has gone by and the news about Leo was still buzzing around town. Squalo did recover from his incident with Leo and could not believe what happened to him. He figured his son would eventually get busted again, but not taken down the way he was.

At first, everyone thought the hit was performed by a drive by shooter or a pedestrian, but the reports were showing the bullet traveled from long range. The bullet used came from a sniper type of rifle and traveled approximately 300 feet, maybe farther.

This changed the investigation since the location of the hit would put a sniper either on a rooftop or on top of another structure in the distance somewhere. This city has never witnessed anything like this in the past. Most incidents were always close range, so it appears to be a planned execution style hit.

Although this was somewhat disturbing to some residents, no one seemed to care since it was Leo that was taken out. Belinda was upset only because Leo was her brother, not for any other reason. She never had a loving relationship with her brother anyway.

Squalo on the other hand, is livid that someone did this to his only son, but there is nothing he could really do except wait until the investigation is complete. He has a few ideas about who could have performed this hit. One person who comes to mind is Nutsy, since years back he was involved with long range rifle shooting.

A few other possibilities could be Papo, Paulie, or even Billy since he was a Marine, years back. No one is ruling out the possibility it could also be a group from downtown, maybe someone retaliating because of Big Charlie, Vito, or even the detective. Leo had formed a list of enemies, so the possibilities are endless.

It's Super Bowl Sunday and Nutsy and Kathy are hosting a party at Sista. Nutsy decided to have an open bar and cater the food again from local merchants. He is a big believer in spreading around his support to local businesses.

It could be just a coincidence, but things have drastically quieted down around the city. Maybe it's because Leo is gone and most residents believe this was a single incident directed at him, so business is continuing as usual.

Miguel decided to withdraw his condo proposal altogether. The pressure from Agent O'Leary and the news about Leo all became too much for him. He has other projects in the works, so he figured this one was not worth the trouble or possibly his life.

Agent O'Leary closed out Big Charlie's case but reminded Miguel to stay clean, or she would gladly reopen it. She believed Miguel was just an innocent bystander at the time and decided to let him see another day.

The atmosphere is much more relaxed at the party and seems almost like the old days when things were in control and moving along smoothly. Nutsy is still patiently waiting for the final approval from the city council. Although Miguel pulled out and most believe it is a given that Nutsy will get his approval, the board has turned down many sports proposals in the past, so nothing is a given.

Billy and Gloria are a hot item now and seem to be the talk of the party since a rumor is spreading that Billy will be proposing to her shortly. In fact, he now asks for everyone's attention. Kathy whispers to Nutsy, "Oh my God. I think he's doing it."

"Good for him."

Billy takes Gloria's hand and guides her toward the middle of the room and says, "I never thought this day would come again but…"

Billy kneels in front of Gloria, pulls out a small box from his pocket, opens it to display an exquisite sparkling diamond pear-shaped ring and asks, "Gloria, will you marry me?"

Billy developed a reputation of being a ladies' man over the years, so everyone witnessing his proposal on one knee is a total shock.

A tear rolls down Gloria's cheek. She never believed this day would happen again after her husband had passed away. Most men are only after her because of her money, but Billy surely captured her heart, and she captured his.

Their relationship is not about money, but a loving companionship that neither one had for many years. Gloria happily accepts and Billy slides the stunning ring onto her finger. It looks spectacular on her and hard to tell what is sparkling more, her eyes or the diamond.

Everyone applauds for this happy occasion and congratulate Billy and Gloria. Nutsy and Kathy decide to let everyone else congratulate them first.

Kathy now hugs her father and then Gloria. She is thrilled to see her father settled in a loving relationship once again instead of roaming around. Nutsy hugs Gloria and then Billy. "Ya did it, ya old geezer."

Billy laughs and says, "Thanks, Nutsy. Come here a minute. I need to tell you something in private."

They both walk to a quiet corner and Nutsy jokingly says, "If it's about the blue pill, I don't take one yet."

Billy laughs and replies, "I'm fine in that department… you did it." Billy smiles.

"Did what?"

"You got the project. Congratulations." Billy holds out his hand for a handshake.

At this point, Nutsy hasn't heard anything from the town or any city official so he's kind of confused and it shows on his face. "I didn't hear a word yet, Billy."

"I know, because I told them I wanted to be the one to let you know."

"Are ya fuckin' kiddin' me?!"

"This ain't April fool's day, Nutsy."

Nutsy skips the handshake and wraps his arms around Billy tightly. A tear forms in the corner of his eye. His plan for his family's future just might be getting closer. At least now he has the nod from the city. "I don't believe it… this might be really happening."

"It looks that way. Come on, let everyone know." Billy slides his arm across Nutsy's shoulders and guides him back toward the family and guests.

After Nutsy announces the great news, the party really kicks into full gear. An engagement and an accepted proposal for the sport park. It is truly turning into a fabulous night.

Nutsy even believes he has a shot to win his Super Bowl box from the Wall Street pool that Tiffany had gotten him into. The pool pays one winner a million dollars.

Sammy and N-J have been sitting together at a café style table. Sammy has been waiting for a return call back from Bono. He has still been staying down South even though his father passed away some time ago.

Sammy notices her phone buzzing and sees Bono's name on the display. She excitedly answers, "It's about time. I was worried about you."

"I'm sorry. I've been really busy down here."

"When are you coming back? I miss you."

"I miss you too… I don't know if I am."

"How come?"

Bono hesitantly replies, "I met up with an old boyfriend."

"You what?" She stands up. This caught Sammy totally off guard.

"It's not you, Sammy, it's me."

A tear rolls down her cheek. N-J notices and starts to fidget with a napkin since not much rattles him up.

"You should be with someone who will give you a hundred percent. I don't know if I ever can."

"But you said you loved me." Sammy wipes away a tear.

"I do, Sammy. But..."

Sammy wipes her tears again. N-J stands up and heads toward Blackie who is close by. "Aunt Blackie, something is wrong with Sammy."

Blackie notices Sammy wiping her cheek with her forearm. She grabs N-J's hand and heads over toward Sammy.

"I promise, I'll come see you as soon as I come back up," Bono says.

Sammy nods and ends the call. She is heartbroken over the news and tilts her head down. She thought they were a couple and had a future together.

Blackie asks, "Do you wanna talk about it?"

Sammy shakes her head no and wipes the tears on her cheek again.

"Come on. Let's get some air," Blackie says and takes hold of Sammy's hand.

"N-J, go find mom. We'll be right back," Sammy says and heads toward the door with Blackie.

Blackie and Sammy are now strolling down the sidewalk. They are both dressed to the nines, so heads keep turning toward them. Blackie has a hunch it could be about Bono since he hasn't been around for a while and asks, "That was Bono, wasn't it?"

Sammy nods but stays quiet.

"Is he okay?"

"Yeah, he's fine… he met up with an old boyfriend."

Blackie always thought their relationship was somewhat peculiar. She couldn't understand how they spent so much time together but never questioned it. "Well, you had to have known that could've been a possibility."

"It's just not fair. We were getting along so well before he had to go see his father."

A straggly man approaches them on the sidewalk and asks for some change. Blackie told him to take a walk.

"He was a nice young man. He just wasn't for you."

"But you don't know how we were together."

"Sammy, his heart leans in a different direction and probably always will. How many times have I said, you are never going to change a person? They have to change on their own."

"But he was changed. I saw it in his eyes."

"Look, you're a beautiful young lady. You will find the right one. Trust me."

"Look at my mom and dad. They've been together since high school and they're still together."

"True but look at me and your uncle. I married him later after many boyfriends. Some I swore I would marry. You just never know, Sammy."

Agent O'Leary walks out of a pizza shop and happens to notice Blackie and Sammy. "Maria!"

Blackie and Sammy both turn to see Agent O'Leary approaching them. "I thought the investigation was over?" Blackie asks.

"Not yet." Agent O'Leary notices Sammy's swollen eyes. "Are you okay?"

Sammy nods and replies, "I'm fine."

Agent O'Leary asks Blackie, "I was thinking, why don't you instruct at my school?"

"Me? An instructor? I don't think so."

"Aunt Blackie, you should do it. You'd be great."

"And maybe you can come and assist your aunt?" Agent O'Leary asks Sammy.

"I'd love to."

Blackie replies, "I'll have to give it some thought."

"And I'd like to take another shot at you. A real match this time."

"Be careful what you wish for." Blackie smiles.

"You beat me by one-point that day. I still haven't forgotten that… think it over." O'Leary walks away.

Sammy asks, "What is she talking about?"

"It was a competition and we had to go head-to-head for the finals. I gave her a spin move at the end and was able to pin her. The funny thing is, she had me beat up until that point."

"Well, you always said. It's not where you start out, it's where you end."

"At least I know you've been paying attention to me. Come on, let's go back. Everyone's probably wondering where we are."

Blackie and Sammy head back toward Sista. They pass by the scraggly man again and he asks for money one more time. Blackie slips him a twenty and says, "If I catch you buying liquor with it, I'll kick your ass."

"No ma'am, not me. God bless you," the man replies.

The party has been going full blast. Nutsy has been downing scotches all night long and Ladro becomes suspicious since Nutsy decided a few months back to quit drinking. Ladro approaches Nutsy at the bar and asks, "I thought you quit?"

"I did. And I started up again."

"So, you don't need to change your ways anymore?" They catch eyes.

"Just ask me what ya want, instead of playin' tiddlywinks."

Ladro laughs and salutes Nutsy. "To the man who had it all figured out."

Nutsy raises his glass and replies, "I'm not sure what you're insinuating, but whatever." Their glasses clink.

"You know this guy was taken down with one shot, right?" Ladro asks.

"Apparently so."

"Long range too. I have to say, that's pretty impressive."

"Yeah, too bad it wasn't you or me that did it."

"I never shot long range, remember?" Ladro is still beating around the bush.

Nutsy peeks at the big screen TV on the wall and says, "Holy shit… if the Boys recover a fumble or interception and score, we'll hit our numbers." Nutsy wants this conversation ended anyway.

Ladro glances at the TV and replies, "You're right, but there's only a minute left. If they recover, the Boys will kill the clock."

"How about an interception runback?"

"Sure, keep dreaming."

A guest in the background yells, "Holy shit! What a pick!"

Both Nutsy and Ladro turn toward the TV. A Boy's cornerback snatched a pass and is now close to going into the endzone for a touchdown. "No fucking way!" Nutsy yells out. He grabs Ladro by the head and kisses him on the cheek.

Ladro's eyes open wide. "No… don't tell me."

"What?" Nutsy asks while turning back toward the TV.

"Another player swatted the ball away. I'm not sure if he crossed or not?"

The refs signaled for a touchdown. Nutsy grabs Ladro by the head again. "Come here ya fuckin' thief." He kisses Ladro on the cheek again.

All eyes are glued to the TV since the call is currently being challenged. Some people in the room have big money on this game so everyone is anxiously waiting for the final call.

The instant replay on the screen shows the runner by the goal line while the ball gets swatted out of his hands by another player. "He's in. We got it," Nutsy says.

Ladro is not convinced the ball crossed the line before being swatted away so he remains quiet.

"Jesus Christ. A fuckin' million, Ladro."

Tiffany, the hedge fund manager, stands next to Nutsy and Ladro and jokingly says, "I hope I get a nice commission out of this." She was the one who got them into the Wall Street pool.

"Let's just wait for the final review." Ladro is still not convinced the ball crossed the line.

Nutsy replies, "I'd be more than happy to give ya a nice tip, Tiffany."

After a minute of waiting for the call to be reviewed, a ref stands in the middle of the field and says, "After the review, the runner never crossed the goal line. Since the ball was swatted out of the endzone, it's a touchback."

"No fuckin' way!" Nutsy yells out and slams his whiskey glass down onto the bar.

Although Ladro agrees with the call, he's still livid about the way they lost. "This is some bullshit... one more yard for a million. I told you they're all a bunch of fucking thieves."

Kathy has no idea what is happening and asks, "What's all the commotion for?"

"Commotion? I'll tell ya what commotion. Ya just lost a million because of a fuckin' hot dog." Nutsy is charged up.

"What hot dog?" Kathy still has no idea what Nutsy is referring to.

"Just forget it." Nutsy doesn't want to get into it and chugs back his whiskey glass.

"Whatever." Kathy walks away since she still has no clue what is going on. And she doesn't seem to care either.

Nutsy says, "I've been bookin' football games my whole life. I've never seen some bullshit like this before."

Ladro replies, "Hey, at least you got the approval."

"Yeah, not that I didn't wanna hit the box, but if I had to pick between the two, it would be the complex every time."

CHAPTER 17

Four months have gone by and Nutsy's project is in full swing. He was finally able to get The Quad's full backing and some low interest financing through the Urban and Planning board. Everyone decided to go ahead with the project since Leo was taken down and things around town got much quieter.

Squalo just sold his condo and is getting ready to head down to Florida. He knows in his heart there is nothing left for him around here. His son was recently executed, and his daughter hates him for taking Leo's side once he had gotten out of jail.

Squalo believes he screwed up royally with Belinda. Leo was just a bad seed, but Belinda did want a better life and has seemed to finally find it. He knows there is no chance for a current relationship with Belinda, but he hopes maybe one day in the future.

Squalo figures he will take his money and start a new venture in Florida. Maybe buy a bar or restaurant. He always wanted to own a top-notch restaurant so now may be his time to.

FOUR SQUARE MILES, *the final project*

Squalo is packed up and decides to stop into The Headquarters to say his goodbyes. Not that he really cares but he wants to explain his thoughts before leaving.

Nutsy agreed to let Squalo in and they are currently sitting in the club chairs by the pool table. Everyone else moved to the other side, including Ladro, to let them talk in private.

Ladro cannot stand the fact that Squalo is here, but he knows Nutsy has dealt with him forever and would feel he at least owes him the benefit of the doubt. After all, Squalo was the one who more or less started Nutsy off with the wager by the bocce ball court.

"You should be proud of yourself, Nutsy. You outsmarted everyone."

"I outsmarted no one. Things just seem to be going my way for once."

"I was wondering. When was the last time you shot at the range or a competition for that matter?"

"At least ten years. Maybe even longer, why?"

"I wonder if you still have the eye, you always had."

"I couldn't tell ya, Squalo. Who knows, maybe one day I'll take it up again."

"Not many could've performed that. In fact, there is only one person around here that had the skill to."

"Nah, it wasn't Billy. He has arthritis in his fingers now."

"I'm not referring to Billy."

"Then who?"

"You, that's who."

Nutsy lets out a laugh and replies, "I know he was your kid, but I'll admit, I wish it was me."

"Who knows, we might never find out." Squalo stands up. He knows his son was a screw up and this could very well get pushed under the rug.

"That's a very good possibility."

"Yeah, good for you. This will make it two, won't it?"

"I'm not sure what you're referring to."

"Sure, you don't… and another thing, I'll be back up for my hundred and eighty-five thousand… and a new fish tank while you're at it."

"I'm out a buck eighty-five also, remember? That was your fuckup."

Squalo glances toward Ladro who happens to be watching them closely with his hand by his belt. "Don't worry, I'm not planning on any moves yet," Squalo sarcastically says to Ladro.

"I hope an alligator chews you into pieces," Ladro replies.

Squalo laughs and replies, "Who knows, a python might just wind up in your house one night."

Nutsy says, "Don't forget the sunblock… now get the fuck outta here."

Squalo leaves and closes the door. Is it the last of him? Maybe, maybe not, Nutsy thinks to himself.

A worker from Sista escorts the plumber's wife into The Headquarters and she immediately wraps her arms around Nutsy. "Whoa, what's this for?" Nutsy asks.

She offers Nutsy a thick roll of cash. "Here, this is the amount you gave me plus a little more."

Nutsy smiles and says, "I never take back money I give out. Never. Buy your daughter something nice."

"You lent me this money, Nutsy."

"It was never a loan."

"I insist, and I don't like to be told no." She smiles remembering Nutsy's exact words when he gave her the money at the cemetery.

Nutsy smiles and replies, "Go see my sister at the bank. Use it to start a college fund for your daughter."

Squalo stands in Agent O'Leary's office and unbuttons his shirt. He rips off wires and hands her the recording device. "Did he confess?" Agent O'Leary asks.

"No, I didn't think he would either. He's not a gloater."

"He said nothing?"

"Only that he wished he had pulled the trigger... am I done now? I wanna get the fuck outta this state. It's been nothing but a jinx for me."

"For now."

"Listen, you told me I'd be cleared if I did this."

"Don't leave the United States. And make sure you give me your new address."

"This is bullshit. Now you're gonna follow me around?"

"You're a part of the family now."

Squalo shakes his head and heads out of her office.

Squalo has all his belongings shipped to the west side of Florida and moves into a luxury home on an inlet. He's still annoyed that someone had done this to his son. In a way, he's not surprised, since Leo was still reckless and never learned from the past.

He tried to say goodbye to Belinda before he left but she just listened to him without replying. He told her everything he did was for her own good and that he is proud of how her life is turning out. She didn't buy it though since her father didn't seem too convincing.

Belinda seems to be settling in just fine with her life. She now works at a bank and is getting serious with a local doctor. A huge change for someone who dated punks and ran Leo's illegal group for a while.

Sammy finally graduated high school and is at Seaside for the weekend with her friends. Nutsy is pacing around the house all night long texting her. Kathy tells Nutsy to leave her alone, but he cannot help himself. This is the first weekend she has ever slept out by herself. Nutsy feels like he'll be losing a few more strands of hair but he knows Sammy is growing up and becoming a young lady.

It's now the end of June and Nutsy and Kathy are hosting a graduation party for Sammy at their house. They decided it would be nice for family and friends to enjoy the summer weather together instead of inside at Sista.

Although it's a sweltering day outside, no one seems to care since a few kegs of beer and a case of wine are being consumed. It's now around 12:30am and everyone is slowly filtering out. It was a fabulous day and Sammy couldn't be happier with how it all turned out.

Sammy thinks about Bono from time to time but understands he must follow his heart. She does believe he loves her but just not in the way she had hoped. In any case, Sammy seems to be getting more involved with the karate school since Blackie had agreed to instruct there from time to time.

The three of them together in a room is a sight to see. Especially when they spar together. Sammy is working her way up the belt colors quickly and is becoming a real contender.

She decided at this point to put her dream of becoming a Seal on hold. She has become more enthralled with the Federal Bureau route since Agent O'Leary has asked her a number of times to consider it.

Agent O'Leary has also become a mentor to Sammy similarly to how Blackie has been all these years. Blackie also told Sammy she believed the Bureau could be a great fit for her. After all, being around her own family has given Sammy more street experience than anyone her age.

Although Sammy always wanted to become a Seal, she decided she wasn't ready to leave the family. Kathy had told her that she needed to be one hundred percent certain and if she wasn't, to hold off until she was.

It's not like working locally when you can decide to change jobs or careers. Sammy understood where her mother was coming from and felt her new direction might be a better fit at this time.

Nutsy seems somewhat torn with Sammy's decision. Although he likes the idea of her not leaving to go out to sea, he is not thrilled she has become friendly with Agent O'Leary who could book him at any time, and possibly, even throw away the key.

Things seem to be moving along nicely with the sports park. The grounds have already been cleared and the structures are being erected. Nutsy told Papo he wants this completed as quickly as possible. He is ready for the next Chapter in his life.

The warmer weather has seemed to help Nutsy's twinges appear less frequently, so he is again, stalling the medical consultation with Munchie. Kathy is still annoyed with Nutsy because of this and decided to take a leave from her job regardless of losing her family's medical benefits. She became tired of listening to his excuses and needed to do this for N-J.

N-J was becoming depressed at the facility and Kathy couldn't take seeing him that way anymore. Nutsy pushed back a little but realized the condition of N-J and knew in his heart, Kathy needed to leave.

Running the sports book and overseeing the project has been extremely stressful on Nutsy, but he figures once the complex is completed, his family's life will change for the better.

Nutsy was on board with Kathy taking the leave for N-J to come home for good, but he is not thrilled with paying the monthly Cobra bill for health coverage. Kathy told Nutsy to suck it up and pay it, and he has been.

N-J agreed to not touch any knives or objects that could be harmful to himself or anyone else. He wants so desperately to be home and believes he can do it. He is getting older and a little more mature, so he is trying his best to not have to go back to the facility.

Belo has finally emerged from laying low and is showing his face from time to time. After the hit on Donnola, he went down South for a while with his wife and Bono.

Agent O'Leary closed out Vito and Big Charles's cases and pegged them on Leo, and rightly so. Donnola's case has been put on the back burner for now since no one seems to care about it. She will eventually get back to it.

The one case that intrigues Agent O'Leary is Leo's. It is not your typical street style hit, and she knows very well whoever performed this must be a master marksman. One bullet used from a long distance is not a fluke. No inexperienced shooter could perform this task even with luck on their side.

Before he headed down to Florida, Squalo told Agent O'Leary that Nutsy used to shoot in long range rifle competitions years ago. Nutsy used to take it up as a hobby before his life became hectic with the kids and business.

Agent O'Leary currently takes a seat with Nutsy at the table they always sit at in Sista. It's like their private table by now. "I wanted to thank ya for everythin' you've been doing for my daughter."

"I see her in me. I'm sure Maria says the same thing."

"Are ya kidding? They're like two peas in a pod."

"I agree. But I gotta tell you, her strength is amazing."

"Yeah, good thing she takes after her mother." Nutsy winks. "So, it's been a while. What can I do for you?"

"I'm still working Leonardo's case."

"I figured you'd have that closed by now."

"Hopefully very soon… so, I understand you were quite the shooter years ago."

"I held my own. Too bad I had to give it up a long time ago… how do ya know?"

"It's my job to know. You held your own?"

"Yeah, that's about it."

Agent OLeary pulls out a sheet of paper and replies, "Well, let's see. Twelve years ago, you won a two-hundred-yard contest. Fifteen years ago, you placed third in a five-hundred-yard competition and second in another the year after. I wouldn't say that's holding your own. I would say that's excellent."

"I had potential. Too bad I had to give it up."

"And why was that?"

"Family, my business. Life gets in the way of things sometimes."

"I'm sure if push came to shove, you'd still have your eye."

"Nah. It's not something ya pick up years later and hit your marks. You should know that. If ya took off a month, would ya hit the same spots?"

"Probably not."

"Imagine over ten years? It would be impossible. Especially long range… I wouldn't even attempt it on a street."

"I have to say, Nuccio, you're a very elusive man. It seems I'm always finding out something different about you all the time."

"Hey, what can I say? Some of us have been around the block a few more times than others."

Time has passed by and the city streets have still been quiet. The Quad has been content and Nutsy's project has been moving along nicely. All the members are on board including Tiffany, who now felt comfortable being able to sell the investment to her hedge fund shareholders. One bullet seemed to have done the trick, at least for the time being.

Belinda and Munchie decide it is time for them to tie the knot and are currently being married by the mayor of the city. Nutsy is standing up for Munchie and Blackie is standing up for Belinda. They are all currently waiting in the mayor's office for her to finish up a meeting.

Nutsy is sitting next to Munchie and says, "I can't believe the potato chip eating doctor is really doing this."

Munchie laughs and replies, "I know everyone thinks our relationship is strange, but we're happy with each other."

"That's all that matters, Munchie. Who cares what everyone else thinks?"

Munchie peeks over toward Belinda who is dressed in a sleek white gown and asks, "She's beautiful, isn't she?"

"Very… just keep takin' the blue pills so ya don't put her to sleep."

Munchie laughs and replies, "Thank you for doing this. It means a lot to me."

"Are ya kiddin' me? I should be the one thankin' you."

The mayor races into the room. "I'm really sorry. The meeting went over time. Is everyone ready?"

Nutsy glances toward Munchie and asks, "Ya ready?"

Munchie nods yes. Blackie looks at Belinda and asks, "How about you?"

Belinda replies, "More than ever."

"Well, let's get you two married," the mayor replies.

The mayor certified their marriage and Belinda and Munchie took a flight to Hawaii for a few weeks. Nutsy volunteered to use his place for a party for them, but they decided to not have one. They were just happy to be married and start their life together.

As crazy as it sounds, Belinda does miss her father and wishes he attended her wedding. She sent him an invitation, but he responded that he could not make it. Squalo is still somewhat bitter about how everything transpired in this city and is not ready to show his face yet. One day in the future he might, but not right now.

Squalo is now involved with an older lady and works at a local racetrack. He hasn't changed much though since he skims a little cash off the track's wagers from time to time.

Sammy decided to start off at a local community college and work part time at the Bureau. Agent O'Leary had to pull some strings to get this done, but she was finally able to.

O'Leary is highly decorated in the Bureau and told her boss that Sammy could be a perfect candidate one day. Her toughness and demeanor are perfect for the job and she is a fast learner. Sammy has also met a nice young agent and has been dating him from time to time.

Blackie is enjoying every minute of instructing at the karate school. The one thing that has been on her mind lately is a child of her own. Seeing the young girls come in to take lessons has made her think of her own situation of never having kids.

It wasn't that Ladro and Blackie didn't want any children, it just didn't seem to be in the cards for them when they had tried to in the past.

FOUR SQUARE MILES, the final project

CHAPTER 18

Another year has gone by and the complex is near completion. A few more final touches and it will be ready for the grand opening. The park looks spectacular with new turf and carved out dirt bases to simulate a real field. Most complexes have turf throughout, but Nutsy wanted the dirt bases since he thought it would separate them from the pack. It also helped save a few bucks.

The bleachers are state of the art with blue foam pads on the seats and back rests. The bleachers wrap around from the right field side to behind home plate. Small bleachers have also been included around the smaller fields for parents to enjoy watching their children.

The two things besides this park that Nutsy is ecstatic about is the home and school to accommodate children with special needs. It wasn't easy getting the school approved through the city and state, but the retired schoolteacher on the board spearheaded the project and pooled all of her resources and contacts to get it done.

A lot of time and effort by many individuals helped get this project to where it currently is and Nutsy plans to somehow pay back each person.

Nutsy is getting close to signing his deal with Binky to give up his sports book. Nutsy feels besides honoring Billy's deal to get out, he doesn't want any interference between the two. This park is totally legit and Nutsy feels the sports book would only hinder its reputation.

At this moment, Nutsy is standing at the same spot he usually stands at. This time he is gazing at a beautiful turfed and spotless field and cannot believe how it all turned out.

Ladro, Papo, and Paulie are sitting at a concession stand table together drinking coffee waiting for Nutsy to join them. They are discussing certain topics that have developed in the city over the past year.

Papo and Paulie both believe Nutsy may have had something to do with Leo's hit. Papo asks, "Ladro, you gotta know something by now. Did he do it or what?"

"I swear. I don't know a thing."

Paulie says, "You're full of shit. You're practically with this guy twenty-four seven."

"I'm telling you. I have no idea. And even if it's true, I have a feeling Nutsy's gonna take this one to his grave."

Papo says, "Well, if it was Nutsy, we gotta change his nickname to The Goat."

Ladro replies, "Yeah okay. Good luck calling him a goat."

Paulie replies, "Not A goat. THE Goat. There's a difference you know."

Ladro replies, "Listen, I don't give a shit if it's A goat, THE goat… it'll never happen."

Papo says, "It's a compliment though. The **G**reatest **O**f **A**ll **T**ime."

Ladro peeks over toward Nutsy who is still gazing at the field. "Does he look like a goat to you?"

Papo replies, "There you go again with, A goat."

Ladro replies, "I'll tell you what, ask him then."

Papo replies, "I ain't asking him. Paulie can ask him."

Paulie replies, "It was your idea. You ask him."

Ladro cuts in, "Enough of this horseshit. He's Nutsy and will always be Nutsy. Fuck that goat shit."

Nutsy finally snaps out of his gaze and heads toward the table. "I'll tell ya, what a score if Binky can get the farm team here."

"They've been in Staten Island for years so… it'll probably never happen," Papo replies.

Nutsy takes a seat at the table and says, "Hey, never say never, right?"

A few more months have gone by and the final touches have been completed on the sports park. Nutsy finally received the C-O on the park from the city and is ready to open for business. There has been a lot of buzz around the area regarding this park, so Nutsy is expecting a busy start.

Nutsy asked Presto to help him with the team enrollments and figuring out the schedules since Presto has been running a team for years in the travel ball circuit. Presto was honored that Nutsy would even ask him, but it was Nutsy who felt indebted to him for even introducing him to the travel ball concept.

The park has a grand brick entrance with a large, curved sign across the top. Pristine concrete paths take you throughout the park connecting one field to another. Nutsy made sure landscaping was included with the proposal. He wants parents to feel at home and relaxed while visiting here to watch their children play ball.

Throughout the past months, N-J took trips with Nutsy to watch the development of the sports park. Nutsy would bring a bucket of hardballs so N-J could practice his pitching against a wall.

Nutsy asked N-J if he could use a sponge ball instead of hardballs since the hardballs kept tearing apart from the constant pounding against the cement wall, but N-J told him it wasn't the same feel or grip.

The cost was mounting up because Nutsy had to order new hardballs every week, but Nutsy didn't care. He was just glad to see his son happy.

N-J would hurl one ball over and over until it split apart and then used the next ball. He has a rubber arm and usually goes through the entire bucket in one visit.

FOUR SQUARE MILES, *the final project*

Billy is currently driving Nutsy and Ladro over to the sports park. The time has come for Nutsy to fulfill his deal with Billy and get out of the rackets once and for all. Billy has been waiting for this moment since Nutsy and Kathy got married and wants to witness it himself.

Billy pulls up in front of the grand brick entrance. The top of the opening has a curved sign that says 'Four Square Memorial Sports Complex' in maroon block letters. The backdrop is gold, and the theme goes with the city's school colors.

Nutsy, Ladro, and Billy walk in after Nutsy opens the gate from a keypad. They all stroll toward a table by the concession stand and take a seat. Nutsy glances toward the concession stand menu and asks, "Ya took the grilled chicken wrap too?"

Ladro replies, "That wasn't me. Your wife made the menu."

Billy takes a glimpse. Next to the chicken wrap it says, The Ladro.

Billy asks, "How did she come up with a chicken wrap being a thief?"

Nutsy replies, "Don't listen to this guy. Within a year, his name is gonna be all over this menu. Trust me."

About ten minutes later, Binky, Belo, and Raymond stroll in. Raymond's eyes open wide while gazing around this pristine park. He remembers playing here himself years back, before making the pros and great memories flash through his mind.

Raymond is one of the few locals fortunate enough to make it as a professional baseball player. He now remains part of the organization as a local scout and has become very friendly with Binky. Raymond and a few of the team's executives meet up at Binky's restaurant weekly since its close to the team's headquarters.

During one of Raymond's lunches, Binky mentioned the park to him and thought it would be a great new home for his organization's farm team.

All three of them approach the table and exchange a handshake with Nutsy, Billy, and Ladro. Binky asks, "Nutsy, you remember Raymond, right?"

"How could I not? He's the only professional pitcher I ever took deep."

"I remember that shot to this day. It might still be going." Raymond and Nutsy played against each other in American Legion one summer.

Ladro chimes in, "Please, his head is big enough."

Raymond laughs and asks, "Is it okay if I take a look around?"

Nutsy replies, "Of course."

Binky says, "And Raymond, it's only about twenty minutes to the main stadium."

Raymond replies, "That's a plus." Raymond walks away. He knows they have business to discuss anyway.

Binky and Belo take a seat, and everyone is ready to get down to business. Since this deal cannot be written on

FOUR SQUARE MILES, the final project

paper, once the final details are agreed upon, it will be conducted with a handshake like back in the old days.

Billy is ecstatic and it shows by his beaming smile. He cannot believe this day is happening. He always dreamed of this day but never really believed he would ever witness it. Binky says, "Alright, so we decided, I'm gonna take the southwest part and Belo's gonna take the northeast section."

Nutsy asks, "You're giving him the money area?"

"I took over Donnola's whole section, so southwest would be easier for me to handle."

Ladro asks, "Shit, ya got Donnola's section too? You're doing alright with this ha, Binky?"

"Hey, I'm no kid anymore. When I buy bananas, I make sure they're not green."

They all laugh and Billy replies, "I know exactly what you mean. I get the darkest ones possible."

Nutsy says, "Alright, so now that we got the bananas all figured out, you're both still good for thirty percent, right?"

Binky glances toward Belo and he nods yes. "Looks like we're all good," Binky says.

"Wait, what's thirty percent?" Ladro asks.

Nutsy replies, "Our cut."

"You mean we're still getting paid?"

Binky replies, "Yeah, every year for nothing."

"For how long?"

Nutsy replies, "Ten years. Merry Christmas."

Billy cuts in, "Can we please get this done already?" Billy just wants the deal sealed before anyone changes their minds.

Ladro wasn't too crazy about giving up the sports book in the first place, but he now feels a lot better knowing they're still getting paid for what they had built all these years. He knew Nutsy had an arrangement with Billy, so he reluctantly went along with it. He is now one hundred percent on board and happy that Nutsy didn't just give it away.

The one area that remains available for the taking is Squalo's since he took off. In the beginning, Squalo tried to run it through texting by changing some code words. It became more of a headache and he eventually gave it up once he got involved with the racetrack.

There was a quick discussion between the men to see who might be interested in giving Squalo's area a shot. The north side of Belo's area is close enough to accommodate The Plains, so Belo said he would accept wagers but only from big players.

Binky says, "I got one request. One of you has to stick around for a while to help make the transition smoother."

Ladro replies, "I'll do it. But I ain't traveling all the way to the Bronx though. It's too far."

Nutsy replies, "Too far? It's the next town over for Christ Sake."

FOUR SQUARE MILES, *the final project*

They all laugh except Billy. Nutsy glances toward him and knows he is impatiently waiting to witness their handshakes. So Nutsy offers his hand to Binky and asks, "Ya ready?"

Binky shakes it and says, "You're gonna do great things here, Nutsy. I feel it. Congratulations."

After Nutsy and Binky shake hands, the rest exchange handshakes with one another and Billy gleams with joy. His son-in-law is finally out. A tear runs down Nutsy's cheek, but he quickly wipes it away. He can't believe his dream is finally coming to fruition.

Billy stands up and asks if he can take a picture of the four of them. They all agree knowing one day this picture will probably wind up on the wall of a restaurant with this story behind it. History is in the making right here.

Raymond finally heads back after taking a glimpse around the complex. He cannot believe how pristine and state of the art it is. He approaches the table and asks, "Are you all done?"

Nutsy says, "All done. Have a seat."

"I have to say, I'm really impressed, Nuccio. If it's alright with you, I'd love to put this place on the list as a future home for our farm team."

"Of course… I don't even know what to say."

"I can't promise anything. The executives make the final call."

Nutsy replies, "I understand. I'm just thrilled you're considering it."

"I got one question though. What are the two buildings on the side for?"

Nutsy glances away for a minute. This park is a dream of his, but the two buildings touch his heart deeply. "One is a home for kids that need special care and the other is a school for them to learn."

"Whose idea was this?"

"Mine."

"I'm impressed. What made you do this?"

Nutsy pauses since this is a personal topic of his and never easy to discuss.

"I'm sorry if I'm intruding," Raymond says.

"Not at all. My boy is autistic. Besides building these fields, I wanted to make sure he'll always have a home with his friends for as long as he lives."

CHAPTER 19

Blackie and Agent O'Leary decide to have their all-out spar. It's early in the morning and they are at Agent O'Leary's karate school. Of course, Sammy wanted to come and watch. She wouldn't miss this for the world.

Blackie and O'Leary decide that kicks to the head are okay but no elbows to the face. Clean punches would be fine but no cheap shots.

Blackie and O'Leary stand in the middle of the floor in their sparring gear. They both have on their black belts and a soft helmet. They bow toward each other and Blackie says to Sammy, "Tell us when one minute is up." Blackie and O'Leary get into their stances.

"Go," Sammy says.

They both dance around a little feeling each other out. Blackie strikes first with a roundhouse to the side of O'Leary's neck. It was a clean strike and O'Leary says," I forgot how quick you are."

Agent O'Leary now turns to throw a kick but spins back with a right-hand punch square onto Blackie's chin that backs her up a bit. It's been a while since Blackie took a punch like this.

"Are you okay?" O'Leary asks.

"Come on… you should know me better than that."

Sammy just smiles. She cannot believe what she is witnessing.

Blackie is ready to go now. She sidesteps, spins, pretends to throw a punch but then quickly comes straight with a kick into O'Leary's mid-section. O'Leary flies into the air and crashes onto the ground. She quickly places her hands behind her head and lifts off the ground with her body, with one fluid motion straight onto her feet.

"How'd you like that one? I worked on it just for you," Blackie says with a smile.

"That would be a nice combo to show the students. But how about this one?" O'Leary spins with a roundhouse kick, smashes Blackie across the head, then squats down with a leg sweep but Blackie leaps into the air avoiding it.

Sammy cannot believe the exchanges between the two of them. Not only are they both stunning in looks and in phenomenal shape, they're both tough as nails. This is truly a sight to witness in person.

Later that day, Nutsy decides to visit the sports park by himself. He is standing in the same exact spot as always. He has been focusing on a certain object about three hundred feet or so away. There is a vibrant red dot bolted onto a tree about six inches in diameter but seems about a half an inch from this distance.

Agent O'Leary heads toward him. Nutsy is currently focused on the red dot and does not hear her approaching him. She just assumes he is daydreaming, but he is intensely focusing on the dot without budging or blinking. He even inhaled and is now holding his breath.

"If I was looking to take you out, you wouldn't be too hard to find," Agent O'Leary sarcastically says.

Nutsy snaps out of his gaze and turns, "I guess it's a good thing we became friends, ha?" Nutsy jokingly replies.

"I wouldn't exactly call us that… you did a good thing here, Nuccio. I have to admit."

"Coming from you, I appreciate that." Nutsy notices one of her eyes are black and some bruises around her mouth area. "What happened to you?"

"I sparred with your sister. No matter what I do, she still has my number."

"She's sneaky, that's why. Are ya here to play ball?"

"You know the case with Leonardo is still open, right?"

"So, I hear."

"You know if I nailed you right now, it would ruin your daughter's chances of ever becoming a Fed."

"Why would ya nail me?"

Agent O'Leary pulls out a long bullet shell from her pocket and asks," Does this look familiar?"

"It looks like the casing from a rifle bullet."

"And happens to be the same caliber used at your competitions."

"So?"

"I found this on a rooftop about a hundred yards out from your business… it had a perfect open sight to it, clear as day."

"It could be a coincidence."

"I think the coincidence is the fact that it also happens to have a clear shot to your house and place your son was living at."

"Now that's definitely a coincidence."

"Yeah, considering it's the only rooftop in the city that is clear to all three locations."

"I thought ya didn't like games, Agent O'Leary?"

Agent O'Leary offers the bullet casing to Nutsy. "Here, you should have it."

Nutsy takes it and replies, "For what?"

"You said the person who did this should have a trophy, right?"

Nutsy hands the casing back to O'Leary. "I told ya already, my trophy days are long gone."

"It's amazing that right after I gave the green light, his head explodes on a sidewalk. Maybe that's a coincidence too."

"It could be or maybe we're both just fools."

"Nah, I always wondered why they called you Nutsy because you're not nuts at all. In fact, you might even be a genius."

"I'm just a high school dropout, that's it."

"I know. Just like a businessman making ends meet, right?" Agent O'Leary walks away.

"O'Leary!"

She turns back and nods.

"So, what's your deal with my daughter?"

"I'm trying to help her out."

"Why, just because you're a nice person?"

She heads back and asks, "It was a long time ago, but do you remember helping a pudgy young girl being attacked by a man in an alleyway?"

"Sure, if it's who I'm thinking of, I beat the shit out of that guy. And really good."

"Yeah, I know you did."

"How do ya know this? That can't be in my file."

"Because you're looking at the pudgy young girl all grown up now."

"No fuckin' way! That was you?"

"It sure was. You were one of the reasons I decided to join the Bureau. To help the good guys."

"I always wondered what happened to that young girl. It was like she disappeared after that day."

"My family immediately moved out of the city."

Nutsy and O'Leary catch eyes. She gives him a smile. "Ya never had any intention of reopening the case against me, did ya?"

"Some hearts are too big to lock up, Nuccio. This city will always need guys like you… just stay good or I'll have your daughter bring you in." She smiles and walks away.

Nutsy chuckles and whispers, "You're really hot shit."

CHAPTER 20

It's opening day of the sports complex and many residents have come out to witness this historical event. The park that was abandoned for years has finally come back to life. Carmela flew up to witness this herself. She remembers bringing Nutsy here to play baseball in the old days and cannot believe what her son has turned this property into.

Nutsy and his family are all close by standing behind home plate. The opening ceremony starts at noon and there is about an hour to go. Raymond and an executive from the farm team head toward Nutsy. Raymond introduces Nutsy to the executive and says, "This guy was the only one who ever took me deep around here."

Nutsy and the executive exchange a handshake while the executive says, "It's my pleasure to be a part of this."

"Thank ya for coming."

"I'm sure Raymond told you our farm team is looking for a new home."

"He sure did."

"We decided, we'd like it to be here if that's okay with you?"

Nutsy's eyes open wide. "Are ya kiddin' me?"

"You can still run your tournaments and operate the facility as you see fit. We would just need practice and game time."

"I'm sure we can figure it out."

"I understand you also have a school and home here?"

Nutsy nods toward the side of the complex and says, "That's correct. The ten-story building is the home, and the two-story building is the school."

"I discussed this with the executives from the main team. They're prepared to give a nice donation to help fund this cause."

Nutsy quickly turns and catches eyes with N-J. He tries his hardest to not shed a tear, but the moment got the best of him. He excuses himself to gain his composure.

The executive says, "Take your time. I heard this is a special day for you and your family."

It's now twelve o'clock and the ceremony has begun. The mayor and city officials are all present. All the big players of the city, including The Quad, are around for this special event and most still cannot believe this day is happening.

Nutsy decided to open the concession stand and offer free food for the event. The names of the sandwiches and wraps are rather odd since most are taken from the nicknames of the residents.

Nutsy promised N-J he could throw out the first pitch, so N-J is currently on the mound tossing a ball back and forth to a man with a catcher's mitt behind home plate.

FOUR SQUARE MILES, *the final project* 223

Raymond brought the farm team catcher along to receive the pitch from N-J. Once he had heard N-J would be throwing out the pitch, Raymond thought bringing the catcher would make it even more special for N-J.

The catcher is now conversing with N-J on the mound. N-J tells him he was a pitcher when he was younger and still practices throwing hard balls against a wall. They are kidding with each other, but N-J says he can still throw gas. So, the catcher tells N-J to bring him his hardest.

All eyes are on N-J while he gets ready. He is not nervous one bit because he knows this is his one and only chance to show his gas, and he has every intention of doing so.

The mayor holds up a mike and says, "Thank you all for coming to this special day. To kick off the ceremony Nuccio Gento Junior will be throwing out the first pitch."

The crowd cheers and N-J smiles back toward them. Kathy wipes a tear from her cheek. N-J winds up and then hurls a blazing fastball on the corner of the plate. Raymond's eyes open wide. "Holy shit! I'd betcha, that was ninety."

The crowd cheers and are now hugging one another. Some residents believe this could truly be the start of great things for this city again. While Kathy hugs Nutsy, he replies to Raymond, "Nah, no way that's ninety."

N-J stands on the mound taking it all in. It is like he is the focus of attention while everyone cheers and hugs one another. At least in his own mind he is and is taking in the moment.

Raymond trots to the mound and says to N-J, "Do me a favor, throw another one." Raymond signals to the catcher, one more.

The catcher squats down and gets in position. Raymond sets his watch to try and time the speed. N-J winds up again and this time hurls one even faster straight down the middle.

"Do you know you throw in the nineties?"

"No, I have no idea how hard I throw."

"Do you throw a curve too?"

"A curve, a change-up, and forkball."

"Let me see your curve."

N-J winds up again and chucks a curve ball that spins from the inside of the plate to the outside corner. Raymond cannot believe the control and speed N-J has. "Son, you have a gift."

Raymond heads back toward Nutsy and says, "I think we found another batting practice pitcher."

"Oh yeah, who?"

"Your son."

"You want my kid to pitch batting practice to your team?"

"Only if it's alright with you."

"Of course. Ya have to ask him though."

"I did already… he said he'd love to."

FOUR SQUARE MILES, the final project

Nutsy glances toward N-J who is showing the catcher the pitches he throws while spinning the ball around displaying his different hand grips.

Nutsy is stumped for words. This was something that came as a total shock to him. "We'll talk later, Nuccio." Raymond heads toward the executive to discuss N-J with him.

Agent O'Leary approaches Nutsy and says, "Congratulations, Nuccio."

"O'Leary, what a surprise. I hope this isn't the day ya decide to bring me in?"

"No, quite the opposite. I'm glad you proved me right."

"And how is that?"

"I had dinner with an old childhood friend. All I heard from her daughter was how her father sent them a guardian angel at his cemetery so they could buy food."

"The plumber's daughter, right?"

Agent O'Leary nods.

"Yeah, I did... I looked at that young girl and she reminded me of the times I had to take scraps from the local store owners to feed my mother and sister."

"Well, you made an impression on them. I heard after she got the insurance money, you wouldn't take a dime back."

"That's right... I told her to see Blackie and set up a college fund."

"And she did."

"Good… I'm not sayin' I did it, but why did ya give a green light?"

"You really wanna know?"

Nutsy nods.

"I thought there was only one guy that had the balls to do it and smart enough to get away with it."

"I thought the case was still open?"

"I'm closing it… good luck here and stay out of trouble." Agent O'Leary winks and walks away.

The ceremony is now over and Nutsy and Ladro decide to have a beer together while sitting on the top row of the main bleachers. From this height, they can see the whole complex and are taking it all in. "Hey, I just want ya to know, I couldn't have done this without you."

"You did it all, Nutsy. It was your idea, your vision, your dream. I just came along for the ride."

"Maybe so, but ya pushed me along. Ya stayed on my ass and made sure I chased it." Nutsy puffs on his cigar.

Ladro's phone rings. "It's Paulie."

"What does he want?"

Ladro shrugs and answers, "Yeah, what's up?"

Paulie sits on his deck overlooking the Atlantic Ocean and asks, "Thirty dozen baseballs fell off a truck on the L-I-E. You guys want 'em before I ask anyone else?"

"How much?"

"Forty cents on the dollar."

"We'll give you twenty."

"Are you kidding? I can get sixty down here."

"We'll take your name off the garlic onion rings."

"No way, I invented those."

"Thirty. Bring 'em up tomorrow." Ladro hangs up.

Nutsy asks, "He got more balls?"

"Yeah." Ladro looks away.

"What's wrong?" Nutsy asks.

"Nothing… I'm just glad you took me in when I was down and out. I'm not saying it was all rosy, but you gave me a life. Much more than I could've ever imagined."

"Ya don't need to thank me, Ladro. You're like the brother I never had."

"Are you ever gonna tell me if it's true or what?"

"Tell ya what?"

"Are you The Goat?"

"I said you're like a brother, not my priest."

They catch eyes and Ladro smiles. They both puff their cigars and gaze toward the field again.

The next day, Nutsy finally decides to go to Munchie's office with Kathy. About a month ago, Nutsy took a blood test. Munchie is currently taking his blood pressure and removes the sleeve from Nutsy's arm. "So?" Nutsy asks.

"It's perfect again."

Kathy asks, "Are you positive?"

Munchie replies, "Yeah, and all the blood work came back fine. The cholesterol is a little high, but we're Italians, right?"

"So, you don't think he has a heart condition?" Kathy asks.

"Nothing is pointing towards it... how have you been feeling?"

"Never better, Munchie. In fact, I feel fuckin' great."

"I guess you're cursing again."

Kathy is relieved that Nutsy doesn't seem to have a heart condition but is still a little concerned. "Why do you think he was getting chest pains then?"

"Indecision."

Kathy asks, "Indigestion?"

"No, indecision."

"Indecision?" Kathy appears confused.

"I'll let him tell you."

Kathy asks Nutsy, "What is he talking about?"

"How the fuck do I know? This guy talks in medical terms all the time." Nutsy knows exactly what Muncie is referring to.

Kathy replies, "I don't think indecision is a medical term."

"Hey, I'm good. That's all that matters."

Later that afternoon, Kathy and Sammy are in the kitchen arranging trust document papers on the island. The papers are currently stacked in piles.

Blackie walks in with a thick binder and places it on the island. "This has everything you need for the family trust, checks, stamps, and details." Blackie races toward the bathroom, "I'll be right back."

Kathy and Sammy curiously catch eyes. They think Blackie's behavior is a bit off. They hear Blackie hurling in the bathroom.

About two minutes later, the toilet bowl flushes again and Blackie heads out of the bathroom. She takes a seat at the island and sighs.

Kathy asks, "Are you okay?"

"Yeah, I think I ate something bad the other day."

"Really?"

"Yeah, really. Why?"

Kathy replies, "If I had to take a guess, I'd say you're pregnant."

Blackie doesn't respond and shrugs.

Kathy asks, "Well, are you?"

Sammy asks, "You're pregnant, Aunt Blackie?"

Blackie hesitantly nods yes.

Kathy says, "Holy shit! I don't believe it." Kathy and Sammy both hug Blackie. They are thrilled about this news.

"Don't say anything. Only you two and Ladro know."

The next morning, Nutsy stands at the same exact spot at the complex intensely staring at the red dot for about a minute. His eyes are focused without even a blink.

A bus pulls away close by and the sound doesn't distract Nutsy one bit. A few kids race by on the sidewalk yelling at each other. Nutsy is still focused on the dot without being distracted.

Sammy pulls up to the entrance in Blackie's car with Blackie in the passenger seat and Ladro in the back seat. "We're here!" Blackie yells out.

Nutsy doesn't budge or take his gaze off the red dot. He inhales and holds it. He starts slowly bending his right pointer finger while still holding his breath.

Blackie yells out the car window again, "Let's go! Some of us have to get to work!"

FOUR SQUARE MILES, *the final project*

Nutsy's pointer finger is now completely bent in while whispering to himself, "Bang." He exhales but still has his concentration on the red dot for a little longer.

Sammy asks, "What is he looking at?"

Ladro replies, "Who knows. Your father has been doing this for years."

Nutsy finally turns and heads toward Blackie's car. "What is it with you, with the staring all the time?" Blackie asks.

"Ya always gotta keep your mind sharp. Ya just never know."

"I think you're losing your mind," Blackie replies.

Nutsy laughs and slips into the back seat with Ladro. "How come Sammy's driving?"

Blackie quickly opens the car door and hurls onto the street. She closes the door. "Shit. Hopefully not again today."

Nutsy asks, "What's wrong?"

Blackie opens the door again and hurls.

Ladro says, "Looks that way to me."

Blackie closes the door and asks Ladro, "You didn't tell him?"

"Tell me what?" Nutsy asks.

Ladro smiles and replies, "You're gonna be a godfather, Nuccio."

"No fucking way!" Nutsy hugs Ladro tightly.

"Yes, way."

"At least we now know ya don't shoot blanks. Come here, ya fuck." Nutsy grabs hold of Ladro's head and kisses him on the cheek.

Blackie says, "And I'm telling you both now, no cursing around the baby."

"Does Kathy know?"

"Yeah," Blackie replies.

"You knew too, Sammy?"

Sammy nods yes.

"Sure, I'm always the last to know everything in this family."

The following week, Nutsy and Kathy decide to have a family Sunday barbecue at their house. Nutsy is currently sitting alone having a beer and smoking a cigar. He is thinking about how fast his kids have grown up and how much his life has changed over the past few years.

He peeks over toward Sammy and cannot believe how mature she has become. The young Federal Agent she has been dating is also present. Of course, Nutsy had to question him when he found out they were a couple.

Sammy doesn't seem to mind anymore that her father questions her friends. She knows her father cannot help himself and needs to be certain of who she is spending time with.

FOUR SQUARE MILES, *the final project* 233

Nutsy now looks over toward N-J who is showing Ladro the grips of his pitches he uses while throwing batting practice to the farm team. Nutsy hopes N-J meets a nice young lady one day to grow old with. For now, he is just happy to see his son settled and content in life.

Nutsy now glances toward Billy and Gloria who are getting ready to elope at a tropical island in a few weeks. They seem like a match made in heaven and Nutsy couldn't be happier for them. Gloria is a generous and caring lady and captured Billy's heart.

Billy peeks over toward Nutsy and gives him a wink. Nutsy smiles and nods back. He takes another sip of his beer and then puffs his cigar.

Nutsy now catches eyes with Kathy who is standing near Blackie. Blackie's pregnancy seems to be going fine and everyone is excited for them. Her pregnancy surely caught everyone off guard.

Blackie has no intention of finding out if the baby is a boy or girl, so she and Kathy have been picking random names. At the end of the day, Blackie already knows she is going with either Nuccio or Kathy but doesn't want to say so yet.

Kathy heads over and takes a seat next to Nutsy. "Why are you sitting here all alone?"

"Just thinking, we could be empty nesters soon."

"It's the right progression in life, Nutsy. I wouldn't have it any other way."

"I agree… hey, maybe I can start chasin' ya around the house again."

"Sure, what a sight that would be."

"Or better yet. I can finally catch the mouse in our house that took my provolone."

"Nah, you're not quick enough anymore."

"Is that right? Talkin' about that, where is it?"

"It's all eaten."

"Yeah sure. Knowing you, ya probably got some trust fund somewhere."

"Yeah right. That's exactly what I have."

Nutsy laughs while Kathy continues, "Look at our kids, Nutsy, where has the time gone?"

"Tell me about it." Nutsy grabs hold of Kathy's hand.

"What's the affection for? It's not like you."

"I wanted to thank ya for puttin' up with me. I know it hasn't been easy."

"You're damn straight it hasn't. But I love you, that's why I did it."

"Yeah… I love ya too, Kathy. Always have and always will." Nutsy takes a sip of his beer then puffs his cigar.

"I can't believe she might become a Fed."

"You? Shit, how about me?"

"It's ironic, isn't it?"

"Not any more than N-J pitching to the farm team."

"Yeah, that's for sure."

"We did it, Kathy. The final project." Nutsy leans over and pecks Kathy on the lips.

"Dad, the steaks are burning!" Sammy yells out.

"I got 'em, Nutsy. Finish your cigar." Ladro heads over toward the grill.

Kathy says, "You two have been together just as long as you and I have been."

Nutsy nods and puffs on his cigar. "Yeah, I know."

"Do you really think this will be the last project?"

"It has to be, Kathy. The next one will be strike three for me."

The End

Thank you for reading the series. I hope you enjoyed it and wish you the best in the future.

Regards,
Keith Michael Preston

Made in the USA
Coppell, TX
28 February 2022